PICTORIAL HISTORY
of
DARVEL

COVER:
Oil Painting of old Darvel
by Hugh Rankin

PICTORIAL HISTORY SERIES

uniform with this book

PICTORIAL HISTORY OF DUNDONALD
R. KIRK — ISBN 0-907526-39-X

PICTORIAL HISTORY OF GALSTON
J. MAIR — ISBN 0-907526-37-3

PICTORIAL HISTORY OF NEWMILNS
J. MAIR — ISBN 0-907526-34-9

PICTORIAL HISTORY OF KILMARNOCK
J. MALKIN — ISBN 0-907526-42-X

© James Mair, 1989

First published in 1989
by Alloway Publishing Ltd.,
Darvel, Ayrshire.

Printed in Scotland
by Walker & Connell Ltd.,
Hastings Square,
Darvel, Ayrshire.

ISBN 0-907526-40-3

PICTORIAL HISTORY
of
DARVEL

James Mair

Alloway Publishing

INTRODUCTION

With the publication of this book 'The Pictorial History of Darvel,' Alloway Publishing's pictorial history of the Irvine Valley is now complete.

When work on the project was started in 1982, little was it anticipated that seven years would be spent in collating and sorting the photographs reproduced in this and in the companion volumes on Newmilns and Galston.

In the compilation of the three volumes care has been taken to avoid repetition of scenes and traditions common to all three towns. These were mainly the events connected with the histories of the Covenanters, the radical weavers and textile production. Also a number of prints have not been published, not because they lacked interest and quality, but because they duplicated a theme already represented. In the end some overlap was unavoidable in the stories of three small burghs situated within a few miles of each other. However each proved to have diverse and in many cases unique characteristics. This was no more apparent than in the case of Darvel.

Darvel came late on the scene as a burgh but the district has a history stretching back to the origins of mankind and in modern times possesses features not often to be found elsewhere.

The unimpressionable attitude to the world by Darvellites was evoked in many stories related to the author, one of which should suffice to illustrate this quality.

Darvel Band, that incomparable group of musicians and wits, was playing at a garden party at Lanfine House after the 1st World War. During the interval many of the eminent guests moved among the players. One was overheard talking to Jimmie Gilchrist, trombonist, who had been in the navy during the war. The subject of the battle of Jutland came up in conversation and Jimmie was heard to say 'Oh, were you there tae' to Admiral of the Fleet, Lord Jellicoe.

Throughout the years of research, assistance was given unstintedly by everyone who was approached, and it became clear that there was still a great interest in the history of each town, of the district and of Scotland as a whole, despite, or perhaps even because of, the superficial treatment which it is afforded in our schools and universities.

It has been said that 'history is the memory of the people.' Naturally, within all our memories there can be at times a slippage of fine detail and slight variations in the recall of dates, but in the feeling for period and in the understanding of human experience the sense of people can often surpass evaluations by academics.

It is a hopeful sign that with interest in locality becoming greater as political and economic decisions are taken ever further away and despite the influences of standardisation and uniformity becoming more powerful, places like Darvel and its neighbours may retain their attractive individuality.

It has been a pleasure and a history lesson in itself collecting material for this book. The author thanks in particular William Anderson who traced a large number of old photographs, Mr. and Mrs. John Girvan and George (Postie) Young for imparting their knowledge of old Darvel and Tom McNaughton for information on the Burgh Band, which seems to require a book of its own. He also thanks J. Stewart McLauchlan, Photographer, Kilmarnock, for the use of copyright material and Hamish Stevenson of Edinburgh for the photographs in all three books on the closure of the railway.

Grateful thanks are also extended to all those listed below for their generous loan of old prints for copying:-

Mrs. A. Allan	Mrs. W. Marshall	Andrew Connell	James Park
Mrs. I. Blane	Miss I. Morton	Robert Croly	David Paton
Mrs. M. Barbour	Mrs. J. Morrell	Michael Cruise	Alex Pollock
Mrs. M. Barrie	Miss J. Provan	John Cuthbertson	Tom Richmond
Mrs. J. Cleland	Mrs. J. Quinn	Jack Dunsmuir	George Robertson
Mrs. F. Crozier	Mrs. J. Richmond	James Frater	Robert Scade
Mrs. J. Dalglish	Mrs. B. Service	Bobby Findlay	Arthur Sharp
Mrs. B. Ferguson	Mrs. Spiers	G. Findlayson	Frank Sharp
Mrs. G. Flemmich	Mrs. N. Strachan	Adam Girvan	Stanley Shields
Mrs. J. Fulton	Miss S. Young	Stephen Hunter	Sandy Stewart
Mrs. N. Gilchrist	Mr. & Mrs. W. Kerr	John Lawson	J.L. Stevenson
Mrs. Graham	Mr. & Mrs. J. Hamilton	Sam Lawson	William Templeton
Mrs. J. Hobson	Mr. & Mrs. J. Muir	James Leitch	George Young
Mrs. J. Ireland	Dr. J.B. Simpson	David McBride	Kilmarnock & Loudoun D.C.
Mrs. J. Kelly	Jim Allan	Robert McBride	Museum Services
Mrs. A. Lawson	George Alston	John Milne	and the Ordnance Survey.
Mrs. J. McDougal	Robert Bramman	Archie Morton	
Mrs. J. McMillan	Andrew Cleland	David Murray	
Mrs. J. McNaught	W. Collins	Bobby Nisbet	

HISTORICAL SKETCH

In 1752 John, 4th Earl of Loudoun, granted twelve feus for housebuilding on ground adjacent to the ancient free-hold of Temple Derval and from this single act the town of Darvel came into being.

The Earl's reputation is founded on his promotion of the peaceful arts, as the creator of modern farming methods in this part of Ayrshire. The pleasant aspect of Loudoun parish on the northern flank of the Irvine Valley, with its farms and woodlands, is the direct result of his agricultural innovations and improvements. But the new system of land tenure had one great disadvantage. This was that now only one family tenanted a consolidated farm, occupying the same area where previously there had been a ferm-toun or a collection of cottages with a number of families.

To overcome the problem the Earl made land available in the villages for the displaced people, or in the case of Darvel created a new village where they could find a livelihood in the rapidly growing handloom weaving cottage industry. In 1727 a Board of Trustees had been formed to encourage the production of linen cloth in Scotland and by mid-century it had become a thriving trade. Parents who could afford to pay the indenture fees to master weavers placed their sons in the craft. In a short time more feus were allocated in Darvel alongside the original twelve and the new village quickly established itself during the wave of prosperity in linen and later silk weaving which lasted into the 1790s, and the cotton weaving boom which followed.

There was a phenomenal growth of the town in its first forty years. By 1791 the parish minister, the Rev. George Lawrie, numbered the population at 400. Prior to 1752 there had been no more than half-a-dozen houses in the vicinity of what is now Hastings Square.

Priestland, in Galston parish, was a larger place before that date, but the artisans of Priestland grasped the opportunity of a move into the quickly growing town. In 1754 Alexander Morton, smith in Priestland Mill, obtained a feu disposition in Darvel, bounded by land already feued by Robert Jamieson, wright in Priestland. This was all part of the movement from the surrounding agricultural land into the towns and into the handloom weaving industry which would sustain the townspeople for another century or more.

EARLY INHABITANTS

Although the youngest of the three towns of the upper Irvine Valley, the district around Darvel yields the best evidence of the ancient peoples who colonised the area right back to the earliest times. The glacial deposits at the eastern end of Loudoun and Galston parishes provided the soil and natural drainage favoured by the first settlers. The upland nature of the countryside, until recently relatively undisturbed by cultivation, quarrying and forestry, has preserved the largest number of field monuments and earthworks.

The most important survivor of these is the Neolithic cairn near Loanfoot farm. It is typical of the Stone Age chambered tombs of the period from 4000 to 2500 B.C. which contained the disarticulated bones of the dead. In its original form it must have been an impressive structure and at 340 feet is regarded as the longest in Scotland.

The scattered remains of another long cairn lie along the west ridge of Hendryton Hill, while further east above the farm of Underlaw are two round cairns of the Bronze Age (2500 to 500 B.C.) These also contained the bodies of the dead, buried singly in stone cists within the cairn and often containing grave goods in the form of pottery and weapons. All the cairns of the district are extensively denuded. They were robbed of stones during the time of the inclosures of land at the end of the 18th and beginning of the 19th centuries for the construction of dry-stane dykes and farm buildings. The people during that period–Scotland's Age of Enlightenment–had lost their superstitious fear of these ancient burial places and reverence for the graves of their pagan ancestors.

The Bronze Age settlers were the Celtic peoples who eventually populated and controlled the whole British Isles, until the Roman occupation, and whose civilization and culture has developed ever since. After 500 B.C. iron tools and weapons were being fashioned and new social structures formed. Hill-forts were characteristic of the Iron Age, but only two small fortified homesteads have been authenticated in the Darvel area, one of these is

Castle Lowrie near Bankhead farm and the other at Wallace's Knowe, east of Loudoun Hill. Many features of early agriculture,–turf and stone enclosures and field-clearance cairns–can still be found at the eastern end of Loudoun and Galston parishes and in neighbouring Avondale. Many are under threat from encroaching afforestation and sand and gravel quarrying. This latter activity removed the most important historical remains in the district.

ROMAN OCCUPATION

The Roman fort by Loudoun Hill was situated on the area known as Allanton Beg, between the road through the Winny Wizzen and the old railway line. It was first surveyed by General Roy in the 1750s and described by the Rev. Robert Stirling, minister of Galston parish in 1837 when the ramparts, gateways and ditches could still be clearly traced. The site had a commanding view eastwards along the route of the Roman road to the larger fort at Castledykes, near Lanark, and westwards towards the Firth of Clyde where possibly another fort was located at the port of Irvine. The Loudoun Hill fort was strategically placed in the territory of the Damnonii, the chief native tribe of this area and according to some writers, in the vicinity of one of the towns of the Damnonii called Vindogara.

First occupied following the advance of Agricola the governor of the province of Britain after A.D.80, the fort was reoccupied and rebuilt subsequently a number of times up until its final abandonment around A.D.163. At its peak as a military station it was probably garrisoned by a cohort of 480 auxiliaries to patrol the road and overawe the natives.

In the 1930s and 1940s small scale sand quarrying endangered the fort. Mr. A.G. McLeod, mathematics teacher at Darvel School, and a leading member of the Darvel Antiquarian and Natural History Society, was instrumental in attracting the attention of university historians and archaeologists from Glasgow and Cambridge. Always vigilant in matters of historical importance to Darvel he recovered a number of Roman artifacts from the working face of the quarry, before a systematic excavation was carried out in the six years after the 2nd World War and before the fort was finally obliterated.

Parts of the Roman road can still be seen between the sites of the forts at Loudoun Hill and Castledykes, but westwards intensive cultivation over the intervening centuries has caused its disappearance. According to the Rev. Robert Stirling it could still be traversed through parts of Loudoun parish, evidence as he puts it that the 'masters of the world' had passed this way. It is surmised that the road from the fort crossed the River Irvine at Passford, rose to skirt the farm of Quarterhouse, descended to cross the Glen Water at the most suitable point, where the present Law Bridge stands, and climbed again to pass westward along the hill slope close to the 500 feet contour. A few exploratory excavations along this line in recent times have found sections of an ancient track. This has at present not been confirmed as Roman, lacking, as yet, the supportive evidence of coins, pottery or other objects, although many Roman artifacts have been discovered over the years in the Irvine Valley.

THE DARK AGES

After the departure of the Roman legions in the 2nd century and until the spread of Christianity among the native tribes in the 6th century (the period known as the Dark Ages) information is sparse. Archaeological finds may yet illuminate some of the historical problems, but until more is available only the contentious testimony of place names can help.

Strathclyde, the ancient kingdom of the Britons, lasted into the 10th century. After 1038 the Scots of Dalriada became the dominant people within an area roughly similar to modern Scotland. Gaelic became the prevailing language for a time over most of the country, requiring a transition from the sister Celtic tongues of the subordinate Picts and Britons. Some of the place names derive from the older Cymric language of Strathclyde. Carlingcraig–the fort of the long rock–stands on the opposite bank of the Mucks Burn from Carnals Castle, a strong defensive position which no longer has any trace of early fortification. Loudoun Hill takes its name from a Celtic deity *Lugh* or *Lleu,* becoming *Lugudunon*–the fortress of *Lugh.*

The name Darvel–the oak wood–is also linguistically connected with the original Cymric with *dar* meaning oak, a tree revered by the ancients, and the Gaelic–*coille,* a wood.

The district around Darvel was an important place in the social, cultural and religious life of the early peoples. It is hardly surprising that a legend attached to the life of King Arthur has local associations. As the military leader of the partly christianised British tribes he resisted the incursions of the pagan tribes of Scots, Picts, Angles and Saxons at a period in the first half of the 6th century. The natural pass over the watershed between the rivers Avon and Irvine at Loudoun Hill, was a route which invading Angles took into Strathclyde. At Glen Water the first of Arthur's great battles was fought against barbarian forces. This was the start of his fabulous and far flung campaigns, the descriptions of which have been recorded and preserved in oral tradition and in written form through the centuries.

While Darvel and Loudoun have their origins in the oldest known languages of the district, Gaelic, which replaced Cymric after the disintegration of Strathclyde in the 11th century, still clings in the names of the upland hills and streams and many of the farms. Glaister comes from *glas tir*–green land; Tulloch is *tulach*–a knoll or hillock; Auchenbart formed from *achadh nam bard*–the field of the poet, or perhaps simply a fenced or enclosed field; Changue from *teanga*–a tongue of land; Cairnsaigh is *carn saidhe*–bitch's cairn; Barbeth from *barr beithe*–birch hill; and Dalquharn, *dail chuirn,*–the field of the cairn. Many others occur, some as hybrids and others Scottisized out of recognition of their original sources in ancient speech.

BARONY OF LOUDOUN

Verification of the historical record accompanies the feudalisation of southern Scotland in the 12th and 13th centuries. Charters, with gifts of land, were issued by the Scottish kings from David I (1084-1153) onward. For these grants Anglo-Norman barons were bound to the service of the monarch in time of war. They in turn ensured support by further gifts from their possessions to relatives and friends.

In the case of Loudoun, Richard de Morville, overlord of Cunninghame, granted the barony to James, son of Lambin in return for the services of one knight. This period saw the introduction of a new style of fortification, the motte-and-bailey, the distinctive defensive work of the Normans which had spread into Scotland. The remains of a number of these still exist in the neighbourhood of Loudoun Castle. The best example, although badly undermined by the Hag Burn, is the old castle of Loudoun near Woodhead farm, with its central mound on which a wooden and later a stone tower stood, surrounded by a ditch and outer bailey.

Firstly the Crawfords and then the Campbells married into the family of Loudoun and consolidated their possessions at the western end of the parish. They gained great influence and power in succeeding centuries as the hereditary sheriffs of Ayrshire. They did not acquire the eastern end of the parish in the vicinity of Darvel until they benefited from the suppression of the Knights Templars in the 14th century and in the aftermath of the Reformation in the 16th century. Many of the old charters giving the boundaries of lands in and around Darvel describe them as part of the old church lands of Loudoun, and some place-names add to the evidence of ecclesiastical ownership. The old pre-Reformation records are lost, but place-names are valuable in having survived in oral tradition until the later documentation of land transactions.

At the eastern end of Darvel lay the kirklands and north-east of these in the valley of the Glen Water a place known as Glen Chapel Holm with a nearby holy well. Nothing remains of a chapel and the holy well has long since been filled in. Most of the land covered by the present town of Darvel and a large area around it were in the possession of the Knights Templars in the 13th century. A house which stood in Temple Street last century was known as Temple Derval and the large extent of the Temple lands can be conjectured from the outlying farms and buildings known as Temple Foulpapple, Templehill, Templehouse and Temple Dalquharn.

THE KNIGHTS TEMPLAR

Darvel's earliest recorded history is linked with the wider world stretching all the way to Jerusalem. The Knights Templars who owned these lands, free of tenure even from the crown, were the Crusading knights, dressed in a white mantle bearing a red cross. Their wealth was derived from estates and farms received as donations from royalty or the nobility. Work on their estates was performed by lay brothers, servants and agricultural workers, or revenue was raised from the rents of tenants. No Templars would be resident in Darvel. Their estate would have been managed on their behalf by bailiffs or foresters and the monies collected used to finance them in their cardinal duty. This was to act as bodyguards for pilgrims travelling from the ports in the Holy Land along the routes to Jerusalem. The farming population in the district around Darvel at that time on both sides of the River Irvine were supporting events far from home. Those in Loudoun parish were providing funds for the Crusading knights. Those in Galston parish contributed to the Monastery of Fail, belonging to the Trinitarian Monks, a third of whose income was intended to ransom Christians captured by Moors while on pilgrimage to the Holy Land.

The lands of Darvel were in the possession of the Templars throughout the whole of the 13th and part of the 14th century, possibly as a gift from the Crawfords of Loudoun. The end of the holy war against the Saracens deprived the Templars of the original reason for their existence. Their vast estates throughout western Europe were regarded with envy and the Knights Templars were suppressed firstly by Philip the Fair, the French king, in 1307, and then in Scotland in 1309 during the reign of Robert Bruce. The Templars had not endeared themselves to the Scots, by taking the part of Edward I of England, who had turned aside from the task of recovering Jerusalem to the conquest of his neighbours the christian nations of Wales, Ireland and Scotland.

In a final decree of Pope Clement V in 1312 the property of the Templars was henceforth to be administered by the Knights Hospitallers, but in effect the lands were gradually secularised and those still in the hands of church passed finally into the possession of the aristocracy at the Reformation–in the case of Darvel to the Campbells of Loudoun. Only Temple Street within the town now reminds us of the earliest recorded owners, while in the countryside, *papple* in Temple Foulpapple refers to the place or fauld of the lay brothers who worked on the Templar estate.

WARS OF SCOTTISH INDEPENDENCE

Although the battle of King Arthur at Glen Water is part of legend, other battles fought in the neighbourhood of Darvel were important historically. The first occurred in 1296 during the career of Sir William Wallace. A number of places in Loudoun and Galston parishes are associated with the patriot, but in Hary's epic poem 'The Wallace' the story is told of his ambush of the English at Loudoun Hill. The poem also tells how somewhere within the parish a hospitable inn-keeper supplied the party of Scots as they prepared to intercept a convoy on route westward to Ayr.

The site of the battle was probably at the eastern entrance to the narrow pass known as the Winny Wizzen. Wallace concealed his men behind the banks and ditches of the long abandoned Roman fort. The poem tells how the Scots made the way narrower still with the construction of stone dykes, making more effective the attack on the tightly packed riders. Fenwick, the English general was killed, his troops defeated and the baggage train, with all the supplies to relieve the garrison at Ayr, fell into Scottish hands.

The point marked on the map as Wallace's Grave is traditionally believed to be the place where the English dead were buried. Wallace pressed on to his great victory at the battle of Stirling Bridge the following year.

In 1307, eleven years after the first battle of Loudoun Hill, king Robert Bruce adopted, almost exactly, the same site and tactics for another encounter with the foreign invader. Modern interpretation places the battlefield further east on the farm of Allantonplains, between the bog land on the north and Loch Gait, now drained, beside the Avon Water. Bruce might well have deployed his soldiers on the advice of veterans of Wallace's army. By digging a series of trenches on either side he further reduced the width of the passage between the difficult terrain of the bog and the loch. This prevented a full frontal attack by the main enemy force of 3000 men and the five to six hundred Scots were able to repulse them. The English fell back in disarray and their commander, Aymer de Vallence fled, abandoning his men to the mercy of the Scots.

Two months later Edward I of England died while on another punitive expedition to the north. Before his death he had shown some regret over his methods of suppressing Scotland, but the barbarity of his earlier campaigns, and by his packing of the country with English judges, garrisons and government officials, had ensured that no amity existed between the two nations, after Bannockburn, for another four hundred years.

Once king Robert I had begun to take full control of his country the greatest change in the district came with the dispossession of the Knights Templars and the re-allocation of their lands. Those others who had also taken the English side were deprived and expelled from the country, while those who had favoured him were rewarded.

The Crawford's of Loudoun had been constant in the Scottish cause. Sir Reginald Crawford, uncle of Sir William Wallace, was murdered by the English at Ayr in 1297. His son, also Reginald lost his life along with his cousin Wallace in 1305. The Crawfords had all along supported Bruce in his claim for the Scottish crown and it was not surprising that Sir Duncan Campbell, who had married Susanna, only child of Sir Reginald Crawford, should be confirmed by Bruce in the lands of Loudoun by a charter of 1318.

RURAL SETTLEMENTS

In the early 14th century the population of the district was still widely dispersed. No villages existed at Darvel or Newmilns. Groups of houses might have been situated in a small kirktoun at old Loudoun Kirk, north of the river Irvine near Galston, and a hamlet at Woodhead for servants and retainers within the ambit of the Old Castle of Loudoun. From that period the estates of Loudoun expanded and by the time of the Reformation the family had become one of the most influential in the west. Large tracts of the country around the Irvine Valley, Mauchline and Muirkirk had fallen into its hands. Having promoted the Reformation, Sir Matthew Campbell in 1566, came into the virtual ownership of the church lands of Loudoun, followed in 1570 by the lands of Loudoun Hill.

Around the period we begin to have a view of the families who lived in the district. Most of the names listed are still found locally and only a few of the places have disappeared:

Johne Auldcorn, Allanetoun,		1571
Pate Broune, Auchenbart,		1572
George Campbell, Lanefane,		1571
Johne Cuik, Loudounhill,		1572
James Currie, Auchenbart,		1572
Johne Fynlay, Tulloch,		1568
Johne Gebbe in ye Glen,		1568
Gebbe Lokhart, Lanefene,		1568
George Lokhart, Greensmill,		1571
Johne Lokhart, Dike,		1568
Johne Lokhart, Rytchartson,		1568
Wille Mair, Tulloch,		1568
John Meikle, Tulloch,		1569
Jon Meytchell, Auchenbert,		1571
Johne Meytchell, Rychartoun,		1569
Johne Meitchell, Coithill,		1572
Johne Maire, Loudoun Hill,		1572
John Nimmo, Byre,		1569
Johne Nisbet, Braidlie,		1571
Sande Pautersone, Tulloch,		1570
Johne Pautersone, Slakis,		1571
Johne Pawtoun, Heidringtoun,		1573
Johne Rychmont, Lanefene,		1568
George Ross, Glen,		1572
Robert Ross, Bankhous,		1572
Johne Steill, Rickartone,		1570
Jok Torrance, Carlincrag,		1570
James Weir, Auchenbart,		1568
Johne Wilsone, Scorecraig,		1571
George Wilson, Bankhouse,		1568
Johne Wryt, Bankhouis,		1570
Johne Young, Allantoun,		1570

More than one surname occurs at each placename as two or three families were grouped in small fermtouns in the old run-rig system of agriculture. The infields were for cultivation. Strips of land were alternately allocated each year to the farmers. The outfield was used for pasture. Peats were cast at the nearest bank on the moorland. It was a co-operative style of farming more essentially so at ploughing time as families had to combine in this difficult operation with up to eight oxen making up a team and pulling a heavy wooden plough. These methods survived into the 18th century in the Irvine Valley, until the agricultural revolution during which the Earl of Loudoun reduced the fermtouns into single unit farms and introduced the rotation of crops, the spreading of lime, field drainage and other improvements.

The names given above along with others not mentioned from the same locations number forty-two. There may have been around fifty families altogether in the Darvel district, giving a population approximating 250-300. A very limited choice of first names, and in the real sense Christian names, were available at that period–two thirds of the males were called John! Darvel's notoriety for nicknames was already in evidence in the 16th century. In the kirk records of Galston and Loudoun parishes, the register of baptisms frequently attaches a byname to some of the superabundant Johns. Johne Pautersone is given an 'alias Storm' and Johne Rytchmont was 'callit Lowrie'.

The girls fared no better with only nineteen variations with Janet outnumbering all the others, which were: Besse, Elspeth, Margret, Katrine, Marion, Nanse, Isobel, Jean, Eling (Ellen), Christeine, Effie, Anne, Sara, Susanna, Gelis, Ame (Amy), Male and Sibell.

Great emphasis was placed by the Reformed Church on the registration of births, which in substance was a record of baptisms. Although the new doctrines maintained that baptism was not essential for salvation, the old beliefs persisted even to Burns's day when among the gruesome items placed 'upon the haly table' by the warlocks and witches in Tam o' Shanter were 'Twa span-lang, wee, unchristen'd bairns.'

The reason for insisting on baptism by the presbyterian church had to do more with church discipline than with the principal articles of faith. The General Assembly of 1616 ruled that every minister was under threat of suspension if he did not have *'ane perfect and formall register, quherein he sall have registrat the particular of every baptisme of every infant within his paroche, and quha wer witness thereto.'* Galston and Loudoun parishes had anticipated this order as early as 1567, but inspection shows an abnormal number of male to female baptisms. This could be explained by careless methods of recording or in the extra importance in noting male births for the purposes of inheritance.

THE COVENANTERS

The Reformation of 1560 fundamentally changed the people in the area around Darvel, many of whom had been tenants on church lands. During the religious upheavals of the 17th century, caused by the determination of the Stuart kings to impose an unacceptable form of ecclesiastical government, they became among the most staunch adherents of the Covenanting cause, especially the hill men of the upland farms. When the adult male population was called upon to sign the National Covenant in 1638, over thirty in the proximity of Darvel attached their names to the section for Galston parish:

Hew Andersonne,	Priestland;
Michaell Baird,	Richardtoune;
Mathew Bordland,	Richartoune;
Johne Broune,	Auchinbark;
Johne Broune,	Bankhouse;
William Broune,	Cairnsaich;
Hew Findlay,	Gorebraeheid;
George Lambie,	Auchenbark;
John Lambie,	Priestland;
Johne Meikle,	Tulloch;
Alexander Mitchell,	Bankhouse;
Jon Mitchell,	Auchenbark;
John, Robert and	
Thomas Patersoune,	Lenfeine;
John Patirsonne,	Tulloch;
James Patoune,	Brocklahill;
George and Thomas	
Ritchmont,	Lenfeine;
John Ritchmont,	Know;
William Ross,	Bankhouse;
Andro Smith,	Ritchartoune;
Archibald Thomson,	Carnsaich;
James Thomsoune,	Priestland;
Johne Thomsone,	Ladybrow;
Hew Wilson, Elder	
and Younger,	Ritchartoune;
Thomas Young,	Coithill;
James, John and	
Thomas Young,	Allantoune.

A similar number signed from the Darvel area in Loudoun parish. They were tenants of John, 1st Earl of Loudoun, who had played a major part in drafting the Covenant, and were parishioners of the Rev. John Nevay a fanatic in the presbyterian cause. Religious controversy was muted during the Cromwellian occupation of Scotland from 1651 until 1660. Detachments of the army under General Monk entered and subdued resistance in the Irvine Valley, but after the restoration of King Charles II the recalcitrant presbyterian party again asserted itself and became a resistance movement whose members were known as the Covenanters.

Throughout the period up to 1689 when the Scottish parliament abolished episcopacy and re-established presbyterianism the people of the Darvel district suffered for their religious beliefs. James Nisbet of Highside was executed in 1684 in Glasgow after interrogation, long imprisonment and cruel treatment. A year earlier John Richmond of Knowe was also martyred in Glasgow after a long term in prison before trial. John Nisbet of Glen had been tried and sentenced to death at Kilmarnock in 1683 for being present at the battle of Bothwell Brig.

But it was at the nearby battlefield of Drumclog that Darvel men made their greatest contribution. When the ministers were barred from their churches the people assembled with them at conventicles, field preachings, whenever they could. These were declared illegal in 1670 and additional troops were raised to suppress the meetings with garrisons placed in parts of the country where loyalty to presbyterianism was strong. A company of dragoons was stationed in the old castle of Newmilns under Captain Peter Inglis. The Covenanters armed themselves for their own defence while attending the open air services.

John Graham of Claverhouse, commander of government troops in south-west Scotland, received information that a large conventicle had congregated near Loudoun Hill. Numbering well over a thousand it demonstrated the strength of the Covenanting support in the Irvine Valley and Avondale, but out of that figure only 250 armed horsemen and foot soldiers could be mustered. The minister the Rev. Thomas Douglas broke off his sermon with the words *'You have the theory, now for the practice,'* and the small army moved off to meet Claverhouse who was approaching from Strathaven.

They clashed at Drumclog on 1st June 1679 and the Covenanters achieved a notable victory. This was their only success until the battle at Dunkeld in 1689, when Valley men were again involved. At Drumclog the extent of Darvel participation is evident in the list of casualties. Only one local man was killed on the battlefield, John Morton of Broomhill, but John Gebbie of Feoch and Thomas Flemming of Loudounhill died later of their wounds. John Morton the Darvel blacksmith arrived during the battle accompanying John Nisbet of Newmilns and was in time to take part in the final advance on Claverhouse and the dragoons. The merciless command in those times on both sides was always 'no quarter,' and Morton offended his comrades-in-arms by sparing the life of a young officer. The sword taken from his prisoner remained in the possession of his family in Darvel until recently.

At the end of this period of government persecution, when presbyterian worship was again permitted, the last conventicle in the district was held near the farm of Yondercroft. Through these most savage times the people of the country had held constant to their faith and in 1689 James VII the last autocratic Stuart king forfeited his throne.

WEAVING TRADITION

After the Act of union in 1707 the countryside settled into a period of tranquillity. The only trade of the district, in woollen goods, suffered from competition with the cheaper English products. But by the mid 18th century one provision of the Treaty, which was upheld, began to change economic and social conditions. Scotland received the sum of a quarter of a million pounds, known as the 'Equivalent' which was to recompense the country for accepting a share of England's national debt and which was also partial compensation for the destruction of Scotland's only colony, situated in Central America. Money disbursed from this fund by the British Linen Company was used to encourage the cultivation of flax and the weaving of linen.

Old records prove the existence of weaving as a specialised trade before that date. As well as a grain mill at Dalquharn there had also been a waulk mill for processing the woollen cloth of the district as early as 1631. In a land transaction of October 7th of that year one of the signatories was *'John Thomsoun, walker in Dalquhairne.'* There was also an *'Andrew Campbell, walker now in Hoillhous, in the lands of Temple Darvell'* in 1638. Later in the century the buildings at Dalquharn were modified from a waulk mill to a lint mill and two more lint mills were erected at Stanners and Ranoldcoup. The last mentioned was traditionally known as the old 'Thwack Mill' from the sound created by the rhythmic action of the machinery in the breaking and scutching of flax in the production of linen thread.

By 1752, the new industry based on this product was already thriving in the neighbouring Valley towns, when the twelve new feus for householders were granted in the village of Darvel. Darvel in contrast to the pre-existing huddle of small farms and cottages quickly expanded into a thriving manufacturing town, which by the end of the 18th century was developing on an ever increasing scale in step with demand. In 1791 out of 344 weavers in the parish of Loudoun 58, all male, were located in Darvel.

In 1792 the population was 400 and by 1819 had reached 700. At this time textile production changed from linen to cotton. In Darvel in 1841 the various trades were distributed thus:-

Male Weavers	267
Female Weavers	61
Clippers	189
Pirn Winders	84
Shoemakers	19
Grocers	18
Sewers	17
Wrights	12
Publicans	10
Masons	8
Tailors	8
Carters	7
Bakers	4
Butchers	4
Sawers	4
Carriers	4
Smiths	4
Surgeons	3
Weaving Agents	2
Teachers	1
Coopers	1
Dyers	1
Flax Dressers	1

By this time the population had almost doubled to 1360. A glance at the figures shows the vast majority of the population was directly engaged in textiles.

Night and day the clack of the loom could be heard in the town.

Survivors of the old woollen and linen trades were 'the dyer' still working at the Townhead and the 'flax-dresser' probably operating at Dalquharn.

All the other trades listed are to be expected in small country towns of this period–with one exception. The 'seventeen sewers' were unique to weaving communities in the west, producing the famous Ayrshire white needle-work.

Women and young girls of eight years and upwards were also required in large numbers at clipping–cutting the floating threads on the cloth to bring out the pattern–before the advent of the clipping mills which were built in the middle of the 19th century. Many women were also employed at pirn winding to supply the full pirns of yarn for the handloom shuttles.

Only a few women were involved in handloom weaving, but as Hugh Ainslie, a visitor to the town in 1822, remarked, this hard physical task was only *'a probationary state most of the mothers of the village went through, but on marrying they generally gave up the "box and bobbins" for a "baby and a blanket".'* His companion on their tour regretted that *'a bonny Ayrshire lassie should, instead o' handling the inwork o' a house, or tripping among the green grass, be condemned to make her bread by such unlo'esome thumping and kicking'.*

Although the volume of trade showed a gradual upward movement over the years all was not sweetness and light. There was seldom a shortage of work, but gluts in the market reduced prices and after the end of the Napoleonic Wars in 1815 there was a downward pressure on wages. Plain goods became the domain of the power loom and the days of the gentleman weaver passed away forever. In 1811 girls of seven and eight years had been able to earn five shillings a week at tambouring and the best weavers up to three pounds. By 1841 a male weaver's wage lay between three and eight shillings a week.

EDUCATION

The provision of education in Loudoun parish goes back to the time of the Reformation and the ideal of the reformers of a school in every parish. Children from the Darvel district had the opportunity to attend school from the beginning of the 17th century. As early as 1601 Mr. Andrew Dalrymple, schoolmaster, was resident in Newmilns and after the Scottish Education Act of 1616 a parish school, with a series of schoolmasters, was located there for a further 250 years. By the 18th century the increase in the number of children and the wide extent of Loudoun parish made it necessary to provide additional private or endowed schools.

The passion for education had already been established among Scots in the previous century with the support and encouragement of the church. It was not uncommon for groups of farmers or artisans, out of their meagre incomes, to employ a teacher for their children. The engagement of John Murdoch by the father of Robert Burns and his neighbours is a good example and something similar must have occurred in the Darvel area. The first mention of a school is in 1732, twenty years before the twelve feus for new residents were allocated in 1752. This was a schoolhouse which existed east of Greenfoot cottage, near what is now Burnbank Street.

In 1781 a new schoolhouse was built with the subscriptions of the villagers and the country people, with the heads of households choosing the master. This schoolhouse was on the south side of Main Street at the west end of the Green. It lasted until 1815 when the Marchioness of Hastings arranged to have the old school replaced with a new endowed one with accommodation for the teacher upstairs. Called Hastings School, it was built in a central position on the south side of the Green which was enlarged and made into Hastings Square. The school building was enhanced in 1844 by the addition of a new tower and a bell.

In the intervening period the children's education struck hard times as the economic standing of the weavers declined. Until the jacquard machine was universally adopted attendance at school was sporadic and of short duration. The parish minister, the Rev. Archibald Lawrie reported to the Education Enquiry for Scotland in 1834 that the handloom weavers in the town made *'harnesses, a kind of work in which each weaver requires a "draw boy" to assist him ... The children who are employed are generally from seven to ten or eleven years of age; this has been the means of reducing the number of children at school very considerably, as the children are removed from school after one or two years attendance.'*

The parish school at that date gave instruction in English, writing, arithmetic, book-keeping, Latin and Greek. The non-parochial schools concentrated mostly on the three Rs, while the Sunday Schools which had sprung up attempted to give reading only beyond the normal religious instruction. The circumstances of the weavers' children had little improved when the Rev. Norman Macleod commented eight years later. The children from the landward district were more fortunate attending from five years of age for a period of around five years. but *'the education in the manufacturing villages is sadly defective. This arises solely from want, not of the will, but of the means on the part of the parents to educate their children. Nothing can exceed the anxiety of the parents in this respect, but they can neither spare their children's work or their wages.'* School fees were about ten shillings a year. This was more than one week's wage for a weaver who might have a number of children of school age.

Education in the town improved when Mair's Free School opened in 1868, financed by an endowment of the merchant, Alexander Mair. Richard Tarbet who had succeeded his father at Hastings School moved into the new school as master. It sufficed for a time, but after the passing of the Education Act of 1872 a new public school had to be erected by Loudoun School Board to bring compulsory education to the children of Darvel, between the ages of five and thirteen. It was erected at the junction of Jamieson Road and West Donington Street and served the community until the rapid growth in population and an extended syllabus necessitated a much larger building. This was built in 1904 and still stands on its present site further up Jamieson Road. Successive generations received the major part of their education there and spent their most formative years in the bosom of the community.

HANDLOOM WEAVING REFINEMENTS

The Valley weavers had made their reputation on a tradition of fine goods and various new methods were adopted to maintain a foothold in the market.

Firstly there was a move into lappets, using an attachment to the loom which provided extra warp threads. Then, invented by James Mitchell, the sewing frame, with its series of tiny shuttles, inserted extra weft thread. Both systems added a small coloured spot or figure to the cloth and saved large quantities of the expensive weft, which would previously have been clipped off. But it was not until the introduction of the jacquard machine into the district in 1838 by Joseph Hood that the trade was saved. By virtue of this innovation the making of fine muslins and lenos continued into the last quarter of the 19th century, keeping a skilled labour force in the district, while other handloom weaving areas fell before the advance of the powerloom. Darvel weavers were soon 'hurrying down to the Hoods, Neils and Mitchells, the jacquard machine builders to have them installed, paying for them at one shilling per week.'

The harness of the handloom now governed mechanically by the jacquard improved the speed of production and allowed the weavers to dispense with their draw-boys, young lads whose job was to alter the sequence of warp threads for every movement of the shuttle. The district quickly developed and became famous for its leno curtains with their beautiful all-over designs. By 1844 the eight shillings maximum of a few years before had become a minimum rising to fourteen shillings a week according to Andrew Lyon, weaver in Darvel, while another said that *'the weavers in the village of Darvel, the greater part of whom have some land, are more sober, more industrious, more healthy and wealthy, than those of the same profession in Kilmarnock and Ayr.'*

The next thirty years was a period of steadily improving trade, interrupted only by the scarcity of cotton during the American Civil War of 1861-65. The population rose from 1,362 in 1841 to 1,729 in 1871, during which time the number of weavers almost doubled from 328 to 633.

GAS LIGHT AND WATER POWER

A considerable advance in amenity took place in 1853 when a gas works was established and was piped to most houses in the town.

The pipe laying was done speedily using a horse-drawn plough to run a deep furrow along the earth pavements. Street lighting by gas followed in 1857.

The River Irvine provided a prime source of motive power essential for agriculture and later for the introduction and continuance of textiles from wool through linen and cotton to lace. There were nine water-driven mills in the Darvel area, seven in Galston parish and two in Loudoun. The seven in Galston parish were the four corn mills at Allanton, Bransfield, Priestland and Greensmill, the oldest, dating back beyond 1571. The other three were built some time in the 18th century when new farming methods greatly increased the yield of corn.

The other three mills in Galston parish were at Ranoldcoup, Dalquharn and Stanners. The first two had been waulk mills which were converted into lint mills in the 18th century, with Stanners, also a lint mill, added later and fed by the same lade as Dalquharn. The presence of three lint mills on the lands of Lanfine points to the patronage of John Brown who built up the estate and the family fortune as a linen manufacturer and banker, encouraging the cultivation of flax and the production of linen yarn.

Darvel Mill in Loudoun parish was also established during the agricultural revolution in the 18th century. Like all the other small country mills it benefited from the extensive cultivation of grain throughout the Napoleonic Wars and up until the repeal of the Corn Laws in 1848 again permitted the import of foreign corn. These afterwards declined in number as improved transport led to more centralised milling. The site of Greensmill became Darvel sewage works, and Priestland Mill was replaced by a private house. Allanton closed at the start of this century. Darvel Mill closed after a fire in the 1920s. For a while only Bransfield survived and towards the end the water wheel provided an early and erratic source of electricity to the farm.

The only textile mill in Loudoun parish in the upper reaches of the River Irvine was Townhead waulk mill. This became the Clipping Mill in the mid-19th century for the finishing process of the vast quantities of muslin woven in Darvel. This was also the site where the first lace machine was installed and provisionally turned by water power before a steam engine was installed to drive it. The essential requirement of the modern lace factories lay in a steady supply of water for their boilers and steam engines and to heat the premises. It was only in the years preceding the 1st World War, when the first factories received power from the Electricity Company in Kilmarnock, that the water resources of the Valley become less important.

EXODUS

There was a small reduction in numbers in the population in the 1881 census. However this did not reflect the disastrous collapse of the handloom weaving industry in 1872-73 and the consequent exodus from the town. In that year the weavers in the Irvine Valley went on strike to maintain the prices for their goods. Before the strike they could obtain sixteen to twenty shillings a week, albeit with a working day from 6 a.m. to 8 p.m. After the failure of the strike only ten to twelve shilling a week could be made on the best quality cloth. By 1877 out of 580 handlooms in Darvel only 230 were working and by the end of the century around a dozen weavers still found employment. They were mostly veterans who could not become accustomed to the stern factory discipline of the new and flourishing lace trade which had been introduced to Darvel in 1875.

In the early 1880s an increase in demand occurred for all classes of lenos, but by that date most handloom weavers had taken up employment elsewhere. *The Galston Supplement* commented that when large orders arrived and prices advanced these did 'not have much effect in inducing men to give up the steady wage of the mill for the precarious chance of the handloom.' Also about this time technical improvements revolutionised the power-loom, allowing colour changes to be made linked to the jacquard machine, fashioning goods which became known as madras. The era of the handloom was virtually at an end.

THE LACE TRADE

Many observers throughout the 19th century had been aware of the threat to the handloom by the power-loom, but no more discerning than Alexander Morton, a weaving agent in Darvel. After studying the mechanism and product of a Nottingham lace machine at a trade exhibition, he was encouraged to raise the finance from his own savings and by loans from friends and relations to install one in Darvel. The heavy machinery and later a steam engine had to be transported by horse and cart from the railhead at Newmilns. After surmounting a number of initial difficulties the first lace machine launched into thunderous activity in the old clipping mill east of Glen Water in February 1876.

Away from the powerful influence of the Nottingham trade union and with the availability of an unemployed work force, already skilled in textile work, Morton was able to undercut his Nottingham business rivals. His shift workers were employed round the clock, six days per week and earned on average eighteen shillings, comparable with the best handloom weaver in better days. No payment was made when machines were idle through breakdown or when requiring changes of webs or shuttles.

Alexander Morton over the following five years made amazing progress as a businessman. He already owned a piece of land east of Ranoldcoup when still a weaving agent. When the old clipping mill proved inadequate for his rapidly growing enterprise he sought land for a new factory. There followed a series of purchases in the middle of the town. In 1876 there was sold *'by James Cleland, manufacturer, to Alexander Morton, Alpha Cottage; Alexander Morton, [his cousin] Hastings Place; Robert Morton, [his brother] Townfoot; and Thomas Scade, Townfoot all in Darvel the partners of the company of Alexander Morton & Company... 15 falls, 33 ells of land–number 6 of the plan of Hastings Square'.* By 1879 the eastmost field of the farm of Hillhead had been purchase by Alexander and Robert Morton from Martha Brown of Lanfine and the mansion house of Gowanbank built on it and completed by September 1880.

BUSINESS BOOM

The conspicuous success of Alexander Morton encouraged others to follow suit, erecting factories and buying lace machines on hire-purchase. Under pressure from the lace manufacturing firms in Nottingham, the loom builders had at first refused to sell their machines outside their own district, but they could not ignore for long an expanding market for their latest wide machines in the Irvine Valley. The first phase of development of the lace industry in Scotland between 1875 and 1887 occurred during a national economic depression and many of the small firms in Nottingham with antiquated machinery had difficulty surviving. At first they tried to defame the Valley manufacturers with accounts of their shoddy goods. *The Galston Supplement* in 1886 commented on a Nottingham interviewer who had 'notably failed in destroying the Ayrshire lace trade with his report so rich with romance and personal incident, the American tariff is a heavier factor to contend with than even Nottingham with its long established monopoly and mis-representation can bring into play'.

Alexander Morton & Company's factory expanded rapidly behind Hastings Square and increased the variety of its products, branching into madras, tapestry, chenille and carpets. Within a few years Stirling Brothers occupied the vacated clipping mill and started production. In 1886 Cleland & Campbell entered the field and in 1887 Alexander Jamieson & Co. By that date fifteen lace and madras factories were in operation in the Irvine Valley with two in Galston and nine in Newmilns where the Browns of Lanfine feued out the level land in Greenholm near the railway station. Many natives of the town who had been forced to leave to find work accepted the first opportunity to return, while newcomers were attracted by the explosion of business activity. The local newspaper reported a housing shortage and advised proprietors of the old handloom weaving shops 'to get such repaired and made into substantial dwellinghouses'.

Before the decade was out Alexander Morton had added substantially to his land holdings as further proof of his lead over his competitors and the exceptional return on capital investment. In 1889 he had disponed to him by Martha Brown of Lanfine 'the corn mill called Greensmill; land called Stanners; land of Temple Dalquhairn called alias Thistley Cruik; land of Richardton called Ranaldcoup with the Thwack Mill thereon and machinery, part of the Temple land of Dervall; the Maillen and lands of Temple Foulpapple at Templehouse which is part of the half merk lands of the church lands of Loudoun'.

It is interesting to note that much of this land was later handed over to the town when the firm of Alexander Morton in 1892 generously gave the Morton Park to the people of Darvel freely and in perpetuity.

The fortune of Darvel and of most of its people at this point in time was inextricably bound with that of its leading citizen. By 1890, although other firms were increasing production and employing additional people, Jamieson's had between 60 and 70 and Cleland's about 50, they were far outstripped by the size and vitality of Alexander Morton & Co. with 700 workers, and in lace goods alone producing 100,000 pairs of curtains per annum.

TOWN EXPANSION

The influx of many more people into the town during this period meant a great deal of house building and whole new streets were created–Donington Street, Burn Road, Campbell Street and Burnbank Street. There was an increase in the social, cultural and religious life of the town too.

During a period of six years no fewer than five new churches were built–no mean feat as each of these were substantial buildings, built by stone masons and craftsmen of the old school and beautifully finished both inside and outside. Prior to this time the first church in Darvel had been an austere meeting house erected in 1785 by the Reformed Presbyterians, direct descendants of the Cameronian Covenanters and rebuilt on the site of the present Easton Memorial Church. In 1883 the Seceeders Church in West Donington Street was built by a break-a-way group from the Reformed Presbyterians. The Seceeders had refused to accept the introduction of the singing of paraphrases during the church service.

New congregations who had previously worshipped in neighbouring towns built their own churches. The United Presbyterian Church in Ranoldcoup Road was built in 1884 and the Easton Memorial Church as it later became was re-built in 1885. The Darvel Central Church as a daughter church of Loudoun Old Parish Church was opened in 1888. Finally there was the Evangelical Union Congregational Church built in 1889.

The Vale of Irvine Almanac for 1881 describes the numerous organisations in existence at that time and gives an insight into the social conditions and aspirations of the community. There were the Co-operative Society (established in 1840), Funeral Society, Good Templars, Total Abstinence Society, and Young Men's Christian Association. Recreational activities were directed through the company of Volunteers, Bowling Club, Curling Club, Horticultural Society, the Library and Brown's Institute. To the great reputation of Darvel bowlers, curlers and gardeners was added the renown of the Quoiting Club, the Junior Football Club (founded in 1889) and the Burgh Silver Band, which, between the two World Wars, was indisputably the best brass band in Scotland wholly maintained and financed by a small town.

The transformation of the place from the time in its existence as a thriving handloom weaving town, through a period when it seemed it might decline into a small rural village and then back again into a prosperous industrial community must have seemed incredible to those who lived through it.

DARVEL BURGH

Yet it was at the bottom of the handloom weaving slump in 1872-73 that a group of optimistic citizens decided to raise the town into a burgh. A number of circumstances had argued for this action. There were difficulties in effective sanitation as the town grew in size and population. There were further deficiencies in the system of public order as the problems of youth unemployment increased and many hundreds of vagrants roamed the countryside disturbing the lives of settled communities. There was very little that two baron bailies appointed by the House of Loudoun could achieve. As early as 1860 John Morton, bailie; William Anderson, bailie; and twelve others petitioned the Justices of the Peace for the county of Ayr, complaining 'that a great number of young men and boys are daily in the practice of playing Ball at the Cross, and other places adjacent, thereby obstructing the highway, often cursing and swearing, and preventing the Inhabitants of the village from following their lawful avocation and comfort'.

The seven men of public spirit who petitioned the sheriff in August 1872 for the town to become a burgh were Thomas Hamilton, weaver; John Fleming, weaving agent; James Richmond, draper 4 West Main Street; John Hamilton, Temple Street; Gavin Cleland, shoemaker 5 East Main Street; Hugh Lawson, weaving agent and Alexander Young, cardcutter. The sheriff adopted their petition on the 5th November 1872 and the first meeting of the council was held in the Evangelical Union Chapel on the 3rd February 1873. The advantage for towns forming themselves into burghs lay in the implementation of the great Victorian public health and burgh police acts. The new council immediately introduced numerous improvements in accordance with these. Most of the early business was involved in the provision and repair of public wells, street lighting, footpaths and drainage, the prevention of slaughtering animals or dumping rubbish in the street and in the maintenance of public order. At the second meeting rates were set at four pence in the pound, and at the third meeting it was decided to form a fire brigade, recognising the danger in the majority of houses still being under thatch.

The council then considered 'a room eleven feet square with a six and a half foot ceiling at Hastings Square was unsuitable as a lock-up for prisoners', but found by October that the Alexander Mair Trust 'was willing to grant a feu at the north gable of Mounthooly for building a constable's house, with a room for Commissioners meetings and two cells at the back'.

Minor misdemeanours were not overlooked by the vigilant Commissioners. The clerk had to 'send a note to Jeannie Findlay that she must immediately cease lodging persons in her house, and that Robert Morton, publican, get his dungstead filled up.' Later, on a less agreeable duty, the council 'agreed that a letter be written to Annie Mair, Galston, for the sum of ten shillings and sixpence, being fees of burying a child had by her.' A delegation was also received of the Rev. Mr. Easton, Darvel and the Rev. Dr. Noble, Newmilns, with a memorial of the kirk sessions asking the court to put a check on Sabbath desecration and drunkenness. It was recommended that the public houses close at 10 p.m. and it was 'resolved that the Constable be asked to keep a sharp look out (more especially on Sabbath days) for the publicans selling drink' out of hours.

By the end of the first year the Commissioners were fully into the swing of things. A sanitary committee had been appointed to look after the footpaths, street lamps, the fire engine and the town's greens which were situated at Matthew Burn, Spout, Townfoot, Townhead and the Cemetery. A new footpath had been laid out on both sides of Ranoldcoup and Hastings Place which required Dagon to be once again moved from its site. The treasurer reported that the income for the year had been £83 and expenditure £75, and with a feeling of satisfaction with its stewardship the council resolved that the assessment for the coming year remain at four pence in the pound.

The new year did not bring good fortune to some, for in January 1874 there was an outbreak of smallpox among the tenants in Mounthooly and 'it was agreed that Mr. Starke (factor of Lanfine) be asked to grant the old house at 'Stennars' for the purpose of washing clothes of those persons suffering from the smallpox'.

The old radical spirit of the weavers appeared again in a request for an extension of democracy to give everyone the vote. Darvel was too far ahead of its time and the franchise remained restricted by statutory requirement to persons with land or property of an annual value of £4 and over.

During the second year of the council's life a new town officer had to be appointed. There were six applications and Daniel Pritchard got the job. On appointment, it was made clear that a town's officer should dress and conduct himself with dignity when on council business. The previous holder was requested to hand over the drum, handbell, ladder and lamp, and the key to the schoolhouse. Mr. Pritchard's duties were to ring the large bell in the schoolhouse at 6 and 9 a.m., and at 1,2,6 and 10 p.m.; to light the lamps and put them out again at 11 p.m. (9 p.m. on the Sabbath). He had also to go round with the handbell and call out the town's intimations, warn all the members of the council meetings, and light a good fire at their meeting place–all for £9 a year. Some complaints were later made by a member of the public of the new incumbent's town crying and he was told 'to make his proclamations more distinct and audible'. In 1878 he was relieved of the inconvenience of ringing the 6 a.m. bell by the horn blown at Morton's mill.

While the Commissioners strove to improve the appearance and administration of the town, they were faced with difficult times. At the election of 1877 only 91 ratepayers recorded their votes.

The new lace industry proved an instant success, but throughout the 1870s it could not develop quickly enough to provide work for all those unemployed by the depression in the handloom weaving trade. Men still left the town to look for jobs, and the council accepted gifts of money from more fortunate Darvel exiles to be distributed among the poor. The traditional pride and independence of the Darvellites however prevented the approval of an offer from Miss Brown of Lanfine to maintain a soup pot in the town as an alternative to their plea for money.

The council in 1879 tried to persuade a doctor to settle in the town. There was only one applicant who later withdrew unless guaranteed £350 per annum, but Dr. Lyon arrived that year on the added inducement of half the parochial board money.

PIPED WATER

In 1890 a gravitation water system was introduced. This ambitious engineering scheme provided the towns people with almost unlimited water from iron pumps erected at 100 yard intervals along both sides of the main street. This was considered a big improvement on the use of the old village wells, but it was quite a number of years before the system was extended to provide water 'on tap' in households throughout the town.

At this time lack of communications and transport were hindering the town's industrial expansion. The rival burgh of Newmilns had jumped on to the lace band-wagon and a number of companies had built factories near the railhead in Greenholm. Darvel Council appealed to the Glasgow & South Western Railway for increased facilities for Darvel. The company's engineer pointed out that there was already in existence a surveyed route to the town, but it was not in a position to extend the track at that time. They then turned to the Caledonian Railway Company to build a line from Strathaven, but it was unwilling to comply. By 1883 the problem had become acute and an attempt was made to establish a horse-drawn bus service from a terminus at the Square to connect with four trains a day at Newmilns station, with the railway company granting an annual subsidy of £20. Mr. Findlay of Newmilns was given the contract, but his occasional non-appearance in time for the early morning train caused great inconvenience. It was not until 1st June 1896 that the rail link was connected and the first train steamed into Darvel at 6.30 a.m. 'to a tumultous welcome from almost the entire population'.

The town's development hastened on to the end of the 19th century. By then a thousand people were involved in the various branches of the textile trade. The enterprising businessmen who had introduced the lace industry to Darvel were her own sons, all of whom had grown up in the ranks of the old handloom trade as agents, warehousemen or weavers.

INTO THE 20th CENTURY

A symbol of the burgh's growing prosperity was the construction of the new town hall in Main Street at the beginning of the new century. A lady speaking at its opening in 1905 commented on the change of fortune of the leading industrialists. *'Today every man you meet in the street is a lace manufacturer. Perhaps, when you last saw him, he was at marbles in the playground with shivery and bulging pockets. Today he is a mill owner, talks of eights and sixteens; of ten points and twelve points and double spools, and lives in a house on the Brae... Tonight ends a chapter and begins a new one. The one that ends began with a boiler that went up the street and over the brig about 1875–not long ago. A bit of a dreamer the man that brought boilers to Darvel, when there was a big wheel and a lade with plenty of water in it. This dream set the whole valley on fire; it is burning yet, furiously, and dreaming became, and still is, in vogue'.*

This view was borne out by the second phase of factory building which had begun in 1895, once again self-financed and recruited from within the community's resources:-

1895	Stevenson, Young & Anderson,
1896	John Aird & Co.,
1900	Morton Aird & Co.,
1900	Blair, Smith & Cleland,
1903	Young & Gebbie,
1904	Morton Brothers,
1905	M.S. Mitchell & Co.,
1907	Stirling, Auld & Co.,
1911	Scade, Smith & Hamilton,
1912	A. Goldie & Son,
1913	James McInnes & Co.,
1914	Morton Sundour.

Three more firms started up after the 1st World War:-

1923	Smith & Archibald,
1925	McInnes Textiles,
1926	Smith & Cleland.

There were also A. Frame and Mair & McCartney the card-cutting firms, Cleland's bleachworks and small textile designing companies.

WORLD LEADERS IN LACE

By the late 1920s and before the depression set in the Irvine Valley lace industry was the largest in the world in the production of lace furnishings.

The earliest Ordnance Survey map of the 1850s revealed Darvel as one long street 'The Lang Toon' running from Dublin Road to Glen Brig. By the early years of the 20th century the modern town was taking shape on lands feued by the family of Loudoun and given names to commemorate them; Donington Street, Edith Street, Countess and Campbell Streets. At the same time the older thoroughfares Ranoldcoup Road, Temple Street, Burnbank Street and Burn Road had been extended uphill or down towards the River Irvine. After the decline in population between 1871 and 1881 numbers rose to over 2,000 in 1891 and over 3,000 by 1901, an astonishing increase in ten years. By the enterprise of its businessmen and the expertise of its people, Darvel led the Valley, as the monument to Alexander Morton on the road by Gowanbank avers, into a long period of industrial fame and prosperity.

The people of Darvel came to have 'a guid conceit o' themselves' with a characteristic style of humour which expressed that feeling, but containing an element of self-mockery. Potatoes grown in Darvel have to be reduced with an axe to get them into the garden shed, and when the parsnips are pulled up 'you can hear the kye rowtin in Australia'. One famous local marksman finding himself out of ammunition fired his ramrod instead, which brought down a string of wild geese and on the rebound he fell and smothered a covey of partridges.

Prosperity and good fortune contain the seeds of their own reversal. As early as 1903 James Morton in an article on the lace trade outlined the problems facing an industry with so many firms in fierce competition. *'While we have been developing our lace looms with all our might so that we can now flood the markets with curtains at one shilling and sixpence a pair, we have been blinding ourselves to the enormous importation of curtains from France and Switzerland of high art merit and good commercial returns... It is all right to produce for the million, but at the same time let us have an eye on the better class articles. It seems to me that far too much of the energy of our district, of its brain and ingenuity have been expanded in a fruitless competition as to who can sell a pair of curtains a penny less than another.'*

This proved the recurring problem in the industry, and co-operation among the manufacturers came late and fitfully. Although suffering the occasional slumps so common in textile production, the local lace trade came through the depression of the 1930s intact. Such was the pride of the townspeople in their product that in the 1930s an annual industrial fair was established known as 'The Lace Queen', when the town's textiles, described in the market as 'Darvel Lace' were exhibited for the commercial world and its consumers. This was also a period when the burgh council began a programme of improvements, enhancing the appearance of the town and providing housing for a population which had doubled in fifty years. The town's boundaries stretched eastward with housing schemes at John Morton Crescent and at the head of Kirkland Road. The outlook was bright as the lace industry began to pick up in the late 1930s.

The period after the Second World War has proved to be a watershed with the old order yielding place to new. The large council housing schemes 'doon the Dublin' and at Hutchison Drive and Paterson Terrace enlarged the town. The quoiting ground which was in use up till this time was eventually closed and was swallowed up by the Lochore Terrace housing scheme. The old curling ponds at the top of Jamieson Road (known also as the 'pond brae' for this reason) fell into disuse and they too are now the site of private housing.

The advance of time and the arrival of TV were the death knell of the Darvel Picture House and even earlier to the cinema which operated in Darvel Town Hall. The Town Hall Cinema was one of the last to make use regularly of the services of the town bellman who would go round the town announcing the coming attractions for the cinema that week.

The Darvel Industrial Co-operative Society which for the first half of the century was the dominant retail and trading force in the town began to decline and in an attempt to consolidate joined the two other valley towns to form Loudoun Co-op.

The achievement of Sir Alexander Fleming whose discovery of penicillin revolutionised 20th century medicine was acclaimed world-wide but also in the town of his birth where memorials were raised in tribute and where he was made a freeman of the burgh.

Educationally the function of the schools in Darvel were altered by act of parliament. Darvel J.S. School which had formerly taught pupils up to 3rd year standard became a primary school with pupils going on to Loudoun Academy which opened in 1970, for secondary education and Mair's School is now a nursery school.

After the Second World War there were still twenty mills in the town, fifteen making lace, three lace and madras, and two madras only, but the dangers were always present for a single industry town. Efforts to bring variety in this field were frustrated as new enterprises felt they could not compete with the 'relatively high wages paid in the local lace and madras factories'.

In the 1950s and 1960s fashion changed, tariffs were introduced or extended and competition increased. The local firms met the challenge by investing large sums in new warp-knitting machinery for the production of goods from synthetic fibres. These still followed the traditional lace forms, but were better suited to the modern market.

By 1973, the burgh's centenary, and within two years of the loss of its independent status, the town had gone through a period of economic difficulty, similar to the problems of the handloom weavers a century before. The industry settled on a smaller base, with a scaled-down work force, but the volume of goods produced by modern methods still vies with the output of the old.

For a while Darvel has been a town in transition, but Darvel is still a textile town and although there are now only four firms in the town weaving terylene window nets and a lesser amount of the traditional cotton lace goods, there are three others making-up curtains, nets, and blinds; there is also one firm manufacturing kilts and tartan goods and a new custom-designed factory producing yashmaks and other specialised textiles for the middle east market.

The clack of the loom can still be heard in the town.

There is considerable house building taking place at present in the town with small sites being built up within the old town, along with more extensive private housing in Burn Road and at the Braes.

A more confident feeling is in the air and with the movement of new families into the town, Darvel is looking forward into the 21st century. In its setting at the head of the Valley it is still a good place to live, so that future generations may be glad to join with the old in saying they were

Derval born and Derval bred,
Derval schuled and Derval fed.

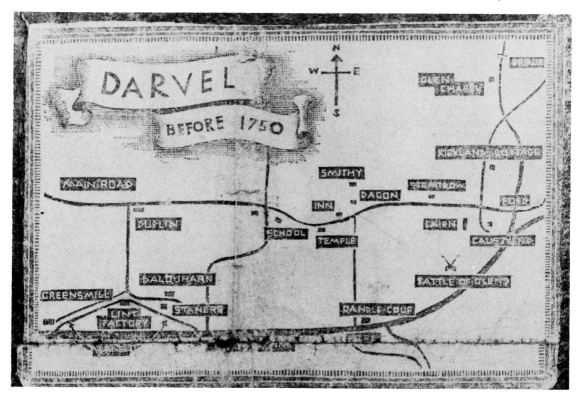

OLD MAP OF DARVEL — All the places shown are known to have existed before 1750, including the prehistoric cairn which lay near the ford where the Glen Water meets the River Irvine. Being drawn from memory some time last century, inaccuracies occur, but all have been described in roughly these locations in various records and memoirs.

LOUDOUN HILL marks the eastern end of the Irvine Valley. From its summit there is an extensive view over Ayrshire to the Firth of Clyde and Arran. The hill has witnessed the passage of history from the earliest times. An iron-age homestead is located at the foot of the south-east slope. Nearby at Allanton Beg a Roman fort was built. Sir William Wallace defeated an English force there in 1296 and King Robert Bruce inflicted greater punishment on the invaders in 1307. A large conventicle held in the vicinity in 1679 led on to the humiliation of Claverhouse at the battle of Drumclog. In the photograph the stretch of road is probably the line of the Roman road, as it left the fort. The old Edinburgh road lay further south. Allanton farm is by the trees on the right and the viaduct carried the line of the Caledonian Railway Company. It was opened in 1905 and for long was a fine monument to the railway age until it was considered "unsafe" and was demolished in 1986 (with great difficulty).

BRONZE OIL LAMP — discovered at the Roman fort on Allanton Beg in 1943 by workmen employed at the gravel quarry. It was presented by A.G. McLeod, the local antiquarian, to the Hunterian Museum of Glasgow University. Many Roman coins were found nearby early last century and in 1803 at Torfoot Farm a coin hoard of around 400 denarii was discovered. The Roman occupation of the fort lasted barely eighty years, before it and the rest of Scotland was abandoned. The defensive line was withdrawn from the Antoinne Wall between the Forth and Clyde to the stronger fortification of Hadrian's Wall.

TEMPLE DERVAL was the house of George Lambie, blacksmith, and was situated on land behind and to the west of Hastings Square (see map on page 20). Built in 1745 the view here is from an old painting. The land was once in the possession of the Knights Templar until the Order was suppressed in Scotland in 1309. The eastern portion of the lands of Temple Derval were occupied at the end of last century by the lace mill of Alexander Morton & Co. The house itself lay part of the way down and across what is now Temple Street, so called to commemorate it and the earliest recorded history of the town. It was taken down around 1851.

HERD'S HORN. Up until the farm enclosures in the second half of the 18th century and first half of the 19th, there were no fields with stone dykes or hedgerows. Cattle and sheep had to be kept away from the crops by young boy and girl herds. They were employed in the ferm-touns and villages and this herd's horn is the oldest antiquity connected with the town of Darvel. It was in use up until the enclosure of the fields and maybe later, moving the villagers' cattle between the small plots of common pasture. The age of the horn has not been determined as the style of circles and zig-zags inscribed on it suggest an earlier date in the 16th or 17th century.

AN OLD SCOTSWOMAN

This print is taken from the oldest portrait in existence of an inhabitant of the Darvel area. Helen Miller married Tom Morton of Ladybrow, one of the large progeny of Mortons still to be found in the district today. She had thirteen children and ninety-four grandchildren. She is seen here in the old style of last century with her shawl and goffered cap. Even her obituary was phrased in the manner of former days when described as a "venerable matron, distinguished during a long life by her industry and hospitality, her piety and benevolence. She left this 'vale of tears' cherishing a good hope through grace".

HANDBELL

Even before Darvel became a burgh in 1873 it had its town bellman touring the streets with public announcements on behalf of the old council of baron bailies and representatives from the town's districts of Toonfit, Toonheid, Toll, Burn and Spout. The bellman was also the bearer of news of local events, visits by the shows or the circus, the latest Co-op dividend, when the water supply would be cut off and restored. Before the publication of cheap daily newspapers he might even mention events of lesser importance, such as the declaration of war and the death of Kings. The photograph shows the inscription "Derval Town Bell 1841".

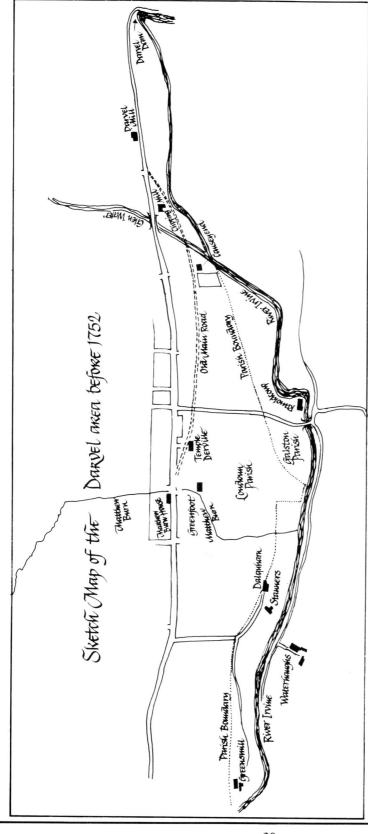

Sketch Map of the Darvel area before 1752.

SKETCH MAP OF DARVEL BEFORE 1752

The line of the present Main Street has been added. The old road, little more than a track twelve feet across, veered south soon after entering the village at the house known as Matthewburn. The twelve new feus allocated in 1752 were on the north side of the road at Cross Street. The construction of a turnpike road through the Valley in the second half of the 18th century ensured the development of Darvel.The importance of the River Irvine is apparent in this sketch map which shows the number of water-powered mills. There were three waulk mills, for fulling cloth, one in Loudoun east of Glen Water later the clipping mill, and the others at Ranoldcoup and Dalquharn later lint mills. These lay in Galston parish and another was added at Stanners, under the patronage of John Brown of Waterhaughs who promoted the cultivation and processing of flax in the district. Temple Derval for generations the farm of the Smith family, by its name retained the connection with the Knights Templar owners of the land in and around Darvel in the 13th century. Other places mentioned before that date are Greenfoot and Causeyend, marked on the map and Straitbow, Damside and Damhead whose sites cannot now be accurately plotted. The boundary line between Loudoun and Galston parishes is shown following the line of the river but with some deviation suggesting that when the boundary line was drawn in the 16th century this was the original course of the river.

A NEW ERA began for the town in the building on the right over Glen Brig in 1875. It is the Old Clipping Mill built on or near the site of an earlier waulk mill. In it Alexander Morton had his first attempt to produce lace on a Nottingham machine using water power from the lade which served Darvel Mill. Proving ineffective, he installed a steam engine and the whole lace industry of the Irvine Valley developed from this. This print dates from the 1900s. The Clipping Mill had become Stirling Brothers and to the east is the new factory of Morton, Aird & Co. On the left is Glen Terrace and further along among the trees is Darvel Mill.

NEAR GOWANBANK, the villa he built in 1880, stands the memorial to Alexander Morton (1844-1923). Erected by public subscription it lies beside the main road overlooking the Lanfine Woods. It was unvieled in 1927 four years after his death in his eightieth year. It is still an impressive piece of work by architect Sir Robert Lorimer containing a bust by sculptor C. Pilkington Jackson and decorative panels of handloom and machine lace weaving. The industry he initiated by his vision and enterprise still survives today with changes in scale and style. It is not yet the end of an era.

THE LANG TOON approached from the west. This view taken at the end of last century shows the road down into the town, possibly soon after the completion of the railway in 1896. The fences and embankments look fresh where the road was raised at the bridge over the track. The first houses are Kilmein on the left and Lintknowe on the right. Lintknowe's name connects it with one of Darvel's early industries, the making of linen yarn from flax. It stands at the head of Dublin Road, at the foot of which the lint was dubbed and soaked in water to prepare it for the lintmill at Dalquharn. Lintknowe is said to have features influenced by the work of the famous architect Charles Rennie MacIntosh. It belonged to William Morton of the Madras firm of Morton Brothers.

THE BIG PARADE led by the Volunteers, reaches the west end of the town. Whether they invaded the neighbouring town or turned at the Dublin is not known. Some of the instruments carried by the Band can be seen in the background. The occasion could have been the Diamond Jubilee of Queen Victoria in 1897 or the relief of Mafeking in 1900, but parades were more common occurrences then in a busy communal life with an abundance of local organisations.

WEST MAIN STREET looking east in the 1890s. The tall building on the right once housed the Townfoot Store of the Co-operative Society. Further along the cottage on the near side of Burnbank Street had the Matthew Burn running under it. On the far corner lived Hugh Black, saddler who had a steady business among the farming community. On the left is one of the oldest cottages still standing (1867). It belonged to Alex MacDougall who drove his cattle through the entry to pasture at the rear. Although one of many in the town officially described as a cow-feeder, he was more generally referred to as someone who "kept kye".

EDITH STREET looking west in the 1890s with only a cottage or two among the fields and trees on the far side of Matthew Burn. Named after the Countess of Loudoun, it is a street of weavers' cottages of a later date. There are more people to be seen than normal in this usually quiet street, excited over the installation of a new gas or water main.

A LONG ESTABLISHED BUSINESS – This shop belonging to John Reid, newsagent and tobacconist, stood at the corner of Burn Road and West Main Street. Replaced by a later building it was still owned by the same family in the same line of business until recently. On the billboards are advertised the popular newspapers the "Evening Times" and the "Weekly News." They tell of great British victories presumably during the 1st World War.

BURN ROAD – By the early years of this century the prosperity of the new lace industry had attracted large numbers back into the town. For a while families could be accommodated in converted loom shops which were part of the handloom weavers' cottages, and there were a few hundred of these. Eventually new houses had to be built like these substantial sandstone cottages in Burn Road. Further up on the left are some new villas and on the right among the trees, "The Braes," home of lace manufacturer Provost Jamieson.

REFORMED PRESBYTERIAN CHURCH — This is possibly the oldest photograph taken in Darvel, showing the old Free Church which was built in 1835. An older church existed on the site from 1785 for this congregation, the oldest in the history of the town was formed by the Cameronians, descendants of the followers of uncompromising Covenanter, Richard Cameron, who refused the religious settlement in 1690 at the time of William of Orange. In 1876 most of the members of the Reformed Presbyterian Church joined the Free Church of Scotland and a new church was built on the site in 1885. It was renamed the Easton Memorial Church in 1894 in honour of the Rev. M.G. Easton who had been its minister from 1861.

THE LAST DAYS of the hand-loom weaver came to Darvel at the end of the 19th century. In 1872 there had been over 600 of them in the town, by the early years of the 20th century there was barely a dozen. In the intervening period when renewed orders arrived for leno curtains few were available to meet them. By 1890 young men were entering the lace mills, but a few old men, before the days of the old age pension, still tried to earn a living at the handloom. The lace firms of A. Jamieson & Co., and A. Morton & Co., employed between 50 and 60 outside in their own loom-shops. Latterly a few like Mr. William Allan in this print found work on jacquard handlooms in separate areas in the factories of these firms. The critical date for the loss of outwork for the handloom weavers was in 1883 when the Beaming House was sold and the members of the Beaming Society were no longer able to use their own machine to prepare their warp beams for weaving. At the near end of the loom can be seen spare shuttles hanging above a clue for collection extra threads from a piece of cloth. On the floor nearby is one of the heavy stones used as a weight for maintaining tension on the warp beam (sometimes they doubled up as curling stones). Beside it is a batch of pirns ready for use in the shuttles.

THE RAVEL SOCIETY — Every warp beamed by the handloom weavers had to be done in the beaming shed belonging to the weavers. It was the only method of control they had over each other on the price offered by the manufacturers. A ravel was an open ended reed for guiding the threads on to the warp beam, the number of teeth depending on the width of the piece for weaving and the fineness of the cloth. The photograph is the first page of the minute book of the Ravel Society showing the names of members and the number of looms owned by each. In 1865 the Society had 268 members including 29 women. They owned 453 looms: 140 with one loom; 66 with two; 35 with three; 19 with four and 8 with no loom. In the hard times during 1872 it apparently combined with the Beaming Machine Society. The minute book was last in the care and possession of the late Mr. Peter Croly, descendant of an original member.

FIRE BRIGADE — One of the first tasks of the new burgh council in 1873 was the establishment of a fire brigade in a very combustible town of thatched roofs. By 1910, the year of this photograph, a fully equipped and kitted-out unit had long been organised, ready to dash to any conflagration from its station in Burn Road. Here they stand for inspection left to right: James Nisbet, William Aird, James Craig, A. Airlie (captain), J. Jamieson, A. Todd (sub-captain) and T. Richmond. They had a pawky sense of humour demanding that "twenty-four hours' notice required to be given of all fires".

LAMMIE'S CORNER – This view from the 1900s is looking east along West Main Street. On the left are the railings in front of the Congregational Church and alongside the house of Thomas Fleming grain merchant and agent of the Union Bank. It was demolished in the 1970s and the site is now occupied by the branch of the Bank of Scotland in a less traditional style of architecture. Beyond the pend and now part of the Black Bull Hotel is the shop of Jimmy Muirhead, barber and pioneer socialist, who combined hair-dressing with public speaking across the road in the Square. On the right at the corner of Temple Street is the outfitter's shop of David Lammie an early exponent of advertising jingles such as:

"Lambie's trousers down again;
Come and see his drawers."

THE TOWN HALL – Darvel was transformed in the late 19th and early 20th centuries during the prosperous times which had arrived in 1875 with the lace manufacturing industry. The small handloom weaving village suddenly changed into a thriving commercial centre. Factory owners' villas appeared on the outskirts, two storied sandstone houses replaced many of the thatched cottages and a crop of handsome stone buildings marked the importance of the town and its trade. The Town Hall was built by public subscription in 1905, looking across to Hastings Square. Thereafter it was the hub of the towns social activity, the venue of the Farmers', the Merchants' and the Tory Ball, innumerable concerts and shows and until after the 2nd World War it served as the town's other cinema. Within its walls the progress of the town was planned ahead by nine local, unpaid burgh councillors, keen to advance the fortune and welfare of the citizens.

THE TOLL

"It happened on a Lammas nicht,
As I gaed oot for a stroll,
I hadnae gaun sae very faur,
Tae I daunered doon by the Toll."

The toll mentioned in the song was situated on Main Street at the head of Ranoldcoup Road. Looking towards Hastings Square, first left, is the Black Bull Inn and barely discernible by the left-hand toll gate, in its original position, is the Dagon stone. Over the roof top on the left the bell tower of old Hastings School can be seen. The first turnpike road through the Valley was constructed after an Act of 1766. The upkeep of the roads was financed by tolls levied at the toll gates on wheeled vehicles and animals, until an Act of 1889 creating county councils passed to them the maintenance of roads and bridges. After that the toll gates seen here would have been left open permanently until finally removed.

TOWN CENTRE — The wide main street looking west at the beginning of this century, before the construction of the Town Hall and after the removal of the Toll gates. Children could play safely on the road until the days arrived when pedestrians would be considered a menace to carefree motoring. On the right is the spire of the Easton Memorial Church, but much is changed east of the Black Bull Hotel. The large building with "Stabling" written on the gable is the site of the Town Hall, and the cottages and shop with the barber's pole are all replaced up to Cross Street corner.

FAMILY LIFE at the beginning of the century usually meant one with large numbers often living in over-crowded conditions in a but and ben or sometimes only an attic. Respectability and a valued place in the community were the aims of all. Clothes and footwear were made to last and the best kept for kirk-going on Sunday or when visiting. Also desirable was a family portrait in a posed photograph taken in a studio with painted backdrop. Saying "cheese" was not one of the accepted parts of the pose and only the mother has a hint of a smile in this Darvel family. Seven children was common enough but this might even rise to twice that number.

COMMUNITY LEADERS were men of talent and substance. This group here is the Industrial Science and Art Executive Committee who set themselves the task of raising funds to build the Town Hall. They are pictured here in 1905 in the garden of "The Braes," home of Provost Alexander Jamieson, in the centre front row. This was an exciting period in the history of the town with a rapidly expanding population and rising importance industrially. It was a time of optimism which lasted until the disaster of the 1st World War.

WORK IN PROGRESS in 1905 with a joiner's squad in a clutter of ladders and scaffolding. They are at work on the proscenium in the final stages of the erection of the Town Hall. Five of the workmen are wearing the traditional joiner's brattie and the long period of construction and size of the building made it more convenient to transfer work benches from the shop to the site.

GRAND OPENING — Hastings Square is crowded with people at the official opening of the Town Hall. Only two small boys at the rear are aware of the cameraman. The rest, apart from the provost and councillors making their speeches exhibit a marvellous collection of bonnets and hats. These mid-Edwardian days were a hat-makers paradise. Down in the right hand corner is a common sight until recent times of women carrying weans in plaids wrapped around their shoulders.

THE ARM OF THE LAW – One of the advantages of burgh status was access to the resources of the Ayrshire Constabulary and Darvel very quickly applied for the services of a town constable. One of the first to be posted there was No. 29 Constable John Milne who kept any unruly elements under control in the 1880s. In the "Regulations for Officers and Constables" in 1887, number 1 states that each had to be "between 21 and 30 years, to stand at least 5 feet 9 inches without shoes, to be able to read and write, to be free of all bodily complaint, of a strong constitution, fit to pass a medical examination and generally intelligent". It would be interesting to know if the 19th regulation of that time is still in force, to report "all cases in which there are holes or other defects in the streets or footpaths". Another John Milne, grandson of No. 29 was one of the last constables to serve at Darvel before the closure of the local police station.

THE TOWN HALL was opened in 1905, erected by public subscription. Its completion marked the end of thirty years of rapid change and economic advance. The clack of the handloom shuttle was rarely heard, but already eleven lace and madras factories were working round the clock. Workers were ferried in from neighbouring towns to the east and west. The town was expanding in an era of prosperity and the new town hall was a fitting memorial to the enterprise of the citizens of the burgh. Before its ceremonial opening a group of the workmen who built it, masons, joiners, plasterers and painters are the first to take the stage.

HASTINGS SQUARE seen here at the turn of the century, was named after the Marchioness of Hastings. Local people also called it the Cross and before being tidied up and planted with trees by the burgh council it had been the venue for visiting shows and town sports with races up and down the street. Early cinema performances were held in a marquee there and the Volunteers made it their parade ground. It had even seen President Kruger burnt in effigy at the beginning of the Boer War but seemed by the date of this picture to have settled down as the meeting place of numerous children and rendezvous of the local cycling club. The corner building on the right became the premises of Walker & Connell, printers and stationers, but had been one of the early shops of Darvel Industrial Co-operative Society established in 1840. The building on the far left corner had been for a while the public house, The Hastings Arms. The public drinking fountain in the centre was presented to the town at the inauguration of the gravitation water supply in 1890.

THE CORONATION of King Edward VII was celebrated at an open-air service in Hastings Square in 1901 after a grand procession. The whole town turned out to watch and to listen to the speeches of the civic leaders who can be seen on the platform which the choir. Drawn up before them is the local Company of Volunteers. The new Quoad Sacra Church, now Darvel Central Church, had been built in 1888 giving a final touch of dignity and style to the Square. It replaced the old Hastings School built in 1814 with a tower and bell added in 1844.

RANOLDCOUP ROAD looking south towards Lanfine Estate early this century. On the left is the Black Bull Inn (not to be confused with the Black Bull Hotel fifty yards away). Beyond it is the impressive Co-operative building dating from 1900, obscuring Irvine Bank Church built in 1884 by members of the United Presbyterian Church. Farther along is the Institute Classroom, originally the Free Church school, but used by a host of different organisations since then. The top of the gasworks chimney can also be seen. On the right is the rear of the houses in Hastings Square. On the corner was the shop of Richard Tarbet, fruiterer and confectioner. He kept his cart in the basement and when about to set out on his rounds he shared, rather inequitably, with his daughter the heavy task of hitching up the cart calling, "You yoke the horse, Aggie, and I'll get oot the whup".

MEN OF MORTON'S MILL — West of Ranoldcoup Road, Alexander Morton built his main factory, covering a large area behind Hastings Square, over to Temple Street, and down towards Mairs Road. By 1890 the company employed up to 700 in the various departments of lace, madras, chenille and carpets, having reached that number from the handful which operated the first lace machine in 1875. This print from the 1890s is of one of the shifts from the lace shed, which at that time operated three daily shifts, six days a week for a wage of twenty to twenty-four shillings for weavers. Some of the veterans sport a beard, but already the trend towards the universal moustache of the Edwardian days is apparent.

BROWNS INSTITUTE faces Hastings Place at the corner of Mairs Road. It still stands but is no longer a memorial to the munificence of the Browns of Lanfine, built to provide recreational facilities, reading and lecture rooms for the people of Darvel. Erected in 1872 by the gift of Miss Martha Brown, the last of the Browns of Lanfine, continuing the tradition of her family who had given out webs to weave to the handloom weavers of the Irvine Valley during depressions. They had also given work to the unemployed, building roads on the estate. One relic of the period was the beautiful thoroughfare "The Broons Road" along the south bank of the river, now sadly neglected. Miss Brown also endowed institutes in Newmilns in 1870 and Galston in 1874.

DAGON

The Dagon stone can be described in a number of ways, in geology as a stone pillar of local olivine; in archaeology as a free-standing monolith dating from the Bronze Age with religious significance; in astronomy with its supposed marking from the same period to determine the seasons; in superstition to bring good fortune to newlyweds by marching three times round withershins at weddings in olden times; and scurrilously by envious people from neighbouring towns as "jist a big stane oot o' the watter". As a diety it has lost its powers by being moved from its orignal postion at least four times and by having a spurious boulder placed on top. Its first known location was in Main street at the top of Ranoldcoup Road. It was an obstruction once the Toll gates were removed and it was resited outside Browns Institute. To accommodate road widening it was moved further into the grounds, seen here with the caretaker John Fiddes. This century it stood for a while in the green at Burn Road and in another shift no doubt to the annoyance of the pagan deities it is now situated in Hastings Square.

HASTINGS PLACE at the foot of Ranoldcoup Road in the 1900s with young and old displaying the dress of the period. The houses on the right have changed little, but the gaswork chimney and the works have gone. Away too is "Stirling Castle" a tenement building which stood on what is now the Bowling Club car park. On the left is the entrance to Mairs Road and beyond it is Mairs Free School. The industrial and commercial activity of Ranoldcoup Road has declined, leaving this area a quiet residential part of the town.

BOYS OF MAIRS SCHOOL — The Trustees of merchant Alexander Mair, by the terms of his will, founded Mairs Free School in 1868 for the benefit of the children of Darvel. Richard Tarbet, a man of many parts, was appointed teacher and remained in the position until his retirement in 1903, latterly in the same building as the headmaster of the Junior Department of Darvel Public School. This photograph from 1891 shows him with his young scholars, some in sailor suits and most· of them in knickerbockers and Eton collars — the style of the period. The numerous and valuable assets in money, land and property of the Loudoun and Galston Educational Trust which administered the local endowments, exclusively for the people of the Valley, were later gobbled up by the larger authorities.

DARVEL BROWN'S INSTITUTE

The following Rules for the working of the Institute and the Library were unanimously agreed upon by the Committee on 14th December, 1899 :---

1. The Institute shall be open daily (Sundays excepted), from 9 a.m. till 10 p.m.

2. The Institute may be let or used for public or other purposes at the discretion of the Committee, but not for more than two nights within any one week. On these occasions the Reading and Recreation Rooms may be closed at 1.30 p.m.; but as far as possible readers will be accomodated in the Conversation Room. Three Days' Notice will be given by intimation on the walls of the Reading and Recreation Rooms.

3. Any person, not under the age of Fourteen years, may be enrolled as a Member, if not objected to by a majority of the Committee, provided he promise to abide by the Rules; but no new Member shall be allowed to vote at any General Meeting till Three Months at least after the date of his admission.

4. Each Member shall pay Sixpence Quarterly for the Institute alone, or Sixpence Quarterly for the Library alone, but Ninepence Quarterly for the Institute and the Library together. The Payment shall be made in advance. Members entering between Quarter days shall pay the proportion due to the end of the current Quarter. The Institute year begins on the 1st of September.

5. The Management shall be vested in a Committee of Eighteen, including not fewer than Two Ministers, elected by the Members at their Annual Meeting. The Committee shall have power to fill vacancies that may occur during the year, until the next Annual Meeting.

6. The Annual Meeting of the Members shall be held on the second Thursday of September. At that meeting the Six Members of Committee whose names stand at the top of the roll shall retire. They may be re-elected, or others shall be elected in their places, the names being then put at the bottom of the roll. The pecuniary affairs of the Institute shall be considered, and its general business transacted. Rules may be rescinded, and new ones proposed, but only on condition that notice of the change proposed has been given in writing to the Secretary, at least ten days before the meeting.

7. The Committee shall elect from among themselves a President, a Vice-President, a Secretary, and a Treasurer. The President shall be the Convener.

8. The Committee shall meet Quarterly, on the second Thursday of September, December, March, and June. Any Three Members of Committee may call upon the President to summon a Special Meeting, by giving him due notice in writing, stating the purpose for which the meeting is desired; but no other business than that specified in the notice shall be discussed.

9. No New Publications or Games shall be introduced without the sanction of the Committee.

10. No Smoking shall be allowed except in the Conversation Room. No Members under the age of Seventeen shall be allowed to use the Conversation Room.

11. No body of Members shall be allowed to monopolize the Games. Players shall give place after one Game to other parties, if requested to do so.

12. Members, after finishing their play at any Game, shall return to the Keeper of the Institute the articles required for it, or they shall be held liable for what is lost. A Deposit may be required to guarantee the safe return of property.

13. In the Reading Room Newspapers shall be given up within Ten Minutes after being asked for by any other person.

14. No intoxicated person shall be allowed to enter any of the Rooms. No Intoxicating Liquors shall be used in any of the Rooms. No Betting or Gambling of any kind shall be permitted. No Loud Talking shall be allowed in the Reading Room. No Swearing, Improper Language, or Quarrelling shall be tolerated in any part of the Institute. No Dogs shall be admitted.

15. Strangers making use of the Institute are expected to contribute to the funds through the box in the lobby.

16. The Public Library attached to the Institute shall be specially under the care of a Sub-Committee of Nine, elected according to the requirements of the Ferguson Bequest——Three Members in full communion with the Established Church, Three with the Free Church, and Three with the United Presbyterian Church.

17. The Library shall be open to Members resident in Darvel on Mondays, from 8 till 9 p.m., and to Members resident in the country district at any time, except during one month in the year, when it may be closed for inspection.

18. Each Member may receive Two Volumes, to be returned within Twenty-One days.

19. Books must be kept clean, and must be replaced by Members if returned damaged.

20. Any Member infringing the Rules of the Institute and the Library shall be liable to expulsion, at the discretion of the Keeper of the Institute, who shall report all such cases to the first Meeting of the Committee thereafter, to which Meeting the expelled Member has the right of appeal.

21. The Committee shall always be ready to receive suggestions from Members of the Institute and of the Library regarding its management, and shall consider them at the first Meeting thereafter.

Walker & Connell, Printers, Darvel

INSTITUTES for working men were endowed in the 19th century by rich patrons to provide places for educational and recreational activities. The Brown's Institutes were a boon to the three Valley towns with their libraries, reading and games rooms. Previously no places were available for these purposes, other than public houses. The stingent rules above are typical of the period.

STEPPING STONES over the River Irvine from Browns Road to Morton Park are seen here soon after the park was gifted to the town by Alexander Morton & Co. in 1897. New paths and stairways have been laid out and children are enjoying a paddle in the river. In the background the marquee probably means that one of the regular evangelical crusades has hit the town. The concrete blocks making up the steps have long ago been washed away. A new footbridge erected further downriver in the 1960s gives access at the bottom of Dublin Road to Browns Road at Waterhaughs.

SAWMILL and DAM. The old mill at Ranoldcoup goes back more than two centuries. It is first mentioned as a waulk mill and then in the 18th century as a lint mill and known for a while after as the old Thwack Mill. When the cultivation of flax and weaving of linen cloth died out at the beginning of the 19th century the mill was converted into a sawmill, operating until the second World War. The remains of the building could be seen until recently until a small group of private housing occupied the site. The dam is still there and fishermen still ply the rod nearby. A group of interested spectators look on in this print from the 1900s. The dam was rebuilt around 1903 when Cleland's Bleachworks was erected on this side of the river.

THE BRIDGE at Ranoldcoup at the beginning of the century with a local lady and her children by the riverbank in Morton Park. This bridge and a similar one in Newmilns give access to "the Broons Road." They were probably built early last century, like the road itself, by the Browns of Lanfine giving access to their mansion house and estate. The only crossings of the Irvine before these were the narrow hump-backed bridges between Newmilns and Greenholm and the old Slacks bridge east of Darvel. The exit of the lade from the sawmill can be seen beneath the arch.

COUNTRY WALKS were numerous and popular around the town up until the time of cheap transport. Townsfolk did not travel far even at weekends and many still worked until late on Saturday. A favourite walk was round the Bankers or by Greenbank to the Priestland. The more energetic would tramp to Laben in Changue Glen crossing the burn by this wooden footbridge.

UNISEX — It is not a new development for male and female to be dressed alike. In the 19th century and up to the time of the First World War boys and girls were often dressed in petticoats until they reached school age. This fetching portrait of a brother and sister taken in 1909 poses the problem of which is which. In fact the two young citizens of Darvel are, on the left Cissie Croly and on the right her brother Peter.

KIRKLAND ROAD early in the century in its sylvan splendour. These are the last houses in the road before leading off into the country and the farms by the Glen Water. On the left behind the trees lies Kirkland Park, home of Alexander Morton, cousin of Alexander Morton of Gowanbank and partner in the lace company. It became a busy road on Saturdays as crowds hurried to the Football Park when Darvel produced its first crop of great players, including Nicol and Alex Smith of Rangers and Scotland. All became quiet again when Recreation Park was opened in 1919 at the other side of town.

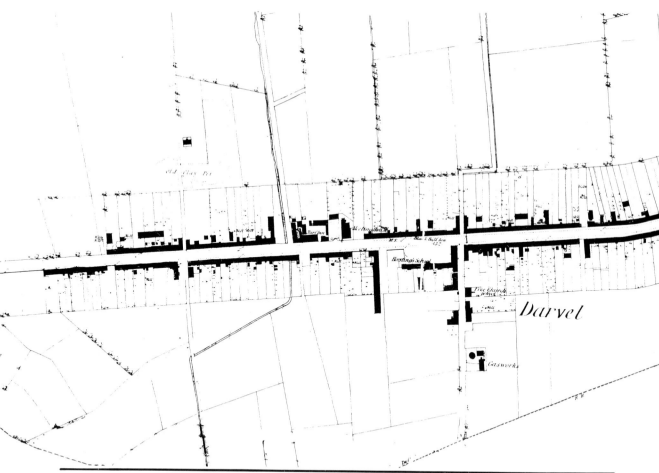

SCHOOL PROCESSION – This print is from 1910 with the school staff and children marching from the school to the town hall at the time of the funeral of King Edward. They are passing Rogerson's shop in East Main Street with the townsfolk looking on. The smart figure of the janitor can be seen near the front. In the early years of public school education he was often an ex-soldier whose tasks included chasing up defaulters and drill instruction to smarten the posture and bearing of the pupils.

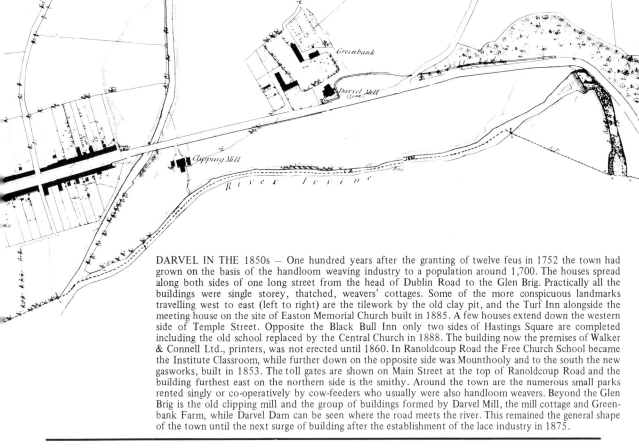

DARVEL IN THE 1850s — One hundred years after the granting of twelve feus in 1752 the town had grown on the basis of the handloom weaving industry to a population around 1,700. The houses spread along both sides of one long street from the head of Dublin Road to the Glen Brig. Practically all the buildings were single storey, thatched, weavers' cottages. Some of the more conspicuous landmarks travelling west to east (left to right) are the tilework by the old clay pit, and the Turf Inn alongside the meeting house on the site of Easton Memorial Church built in 1885. A few houses extend down the western side of Temple Street. Opposite the Black Bull Inn only two sides of Hastings Square are completed including the old school replaced by the Central Church in 1888. The building now the premises of Walker & Connell Ltd., printers, was not erected until 1860. In Ranoldcoup Road the Free Church School became the Institute Classroom, while further down on the opposite side was Mounthooly and to the south the new gasworks, built in 1853. The toll gates are shown on Main Street at the top of Ranoldcoup Road and the building furthest east on the northern side is the smithy. Around the town are the numerous small parks rented singly or co-operatively by cow-feeders who usually were also handloom weavers. Beyond the Glen Brig is the old clipping mill and the group of buildings formed by Darvel Mill, the mill cottage and Greenbank Farm, while Darvel Dam can be seen where the road meets the river. This remained the general shape of the town until the next surge of building after the establishment of the lace industry in 1875.

FIRE AT THE TOWNHEAD — House fires were a more common occurrence in olden days when roofs were thatched and everyone burned coal fires. Thatch often caught fire from sparks from the chimneys and the volunteer fire brigade had to rush to the scene. The Darvel fire engine can be seen in the foreground with a fireman at the hydrant. Another intrepid member of the brigade can be glimpsed through the smoke at the chimneyhead. Large numbers were soon in attendance at these events. In the left hand corner some ladies are looking at the thatch of the adjacent cottage fearful of the fire spreading. All is taking place in East Main Street early this century.

LANFINE HOUSE. The new mansion house of the Browns of Waterhaughs was built in 1772 by John Brown, son of Nicol Brown surgeon in Newmilns and Marion Campbell of Waterhaughs. He had made his fortune as a textile manufacturer and banker in Glasgow reaching some eminence as a bailie in that city. He bought back the maternal estate of Waterhaughs and by 1769 around 400 acres at Lanfine. Born in 1729 he had been apprenticed as a weaver with Alexander Blair of Galston recording in his diary that "a great many gentlemen's sons went to that business about this time as the making of fine linens and hollands was beginning to be introduced into Scotland". This is a recent photograph. The central and original part was built for Brown by James Armour of Mauchline who was to become the father-in-law of Robert Burns.

THE TEMPLE. Up until the death of Miss Martha Brown in 1897 in her ninetieth year, the family over a century and a half had extended Lanfine Estate to over 10,000 acres. The land was improved and woodlands with many exotic trees planted. Roads and bridges were built and many pleasant walks and arbours created within the policies of Lanfine House. In this print from the 1890s the bridge approaching the house from Darvel was built in 1823. On the far side, the area now heavily blanketed with mature trees, can be seen a summer house known to locals as the Temple. The six pillars on the facade originally held up the gallery in the old Loudoun Parish Church, demolished in 1844. The Temple became ruinous during the Second World War and disintegrated soon afterwards. The estate was later in the possession of Lord Rotherwick, and between the two world wars many fetes, garden parties and band concerts were held in the grounds.

GREENHOUSES at Lanfine at the end of last century when castles and country houses were still maintained in lordly magnificence. Labour was cheap and the terrible Liberal politician Lloyd George had yet to increase severely taxes on inherited wealth which would reduce the splendour of families living in country estates. At Lanfine the beautiful woodlands remain, but the pathways, small bridges, rustic seats and follies have now disappeared like the greenhouses in the walled garden or are in an advanced state of decay.

DONINGTON STREET in the 1900s was a quiet residential street towards the eastern end. On the left is the manse and church of the Seceeders whose minister last century was the Rev. Mr. W.W. Speirs, reputed to be the original of J.M. Barrie's "Little Minister." Two buildings along from the church is the old Darvel public school, predecessor of the present one. It was while attending this school that the incident occurred in which Sir Alexander Fleming broke his nose in collision with another boy. The street has not changed much apart from the loss of the iron railings during the 2nd World War, and the presence as in all today's streets of numerous moving and stationary vehicles.

DARVEL FROM THE SOUTH — This is a view of the town before the coming of the railway. Most of the old cottages in Main Street are still thatched, but already new two storied buildings have appeared among them and slate-roofed houses in Burnbank Street and Edith Street. On the far side of town only "The Braes" the home of Provost Alexander Jamieson, lace manufacturer, stands out in splendid isolation. The area east of Burn Road was known as the yaird-heids where the numerous cow-feeders in Darvel rented small parks from Loudoun Estate. Close inspection reveals the newly built churches. From the left is the

THE NEW SCHOOL — The fashion in the early days of school photographs was to scowl at the camera, even for this happy band of Darvel youngsters. Along with their teachers Miss Jean Struthers and Miss Isa Caldwell they are celebrating the winning of the banner as the week's best class. Third from the right in the second row is John Girvan one of the early beneficiaries of education at the new school.

Easton Memorial (1885); the E.U. Congregational (1889): Darvel Central (1888) and Irvine Bank (1884). On the extreme left is the lace factory of Cleland Campbell & Co. At the foot of the hill in Burn Road is Alexander Jamieson & Co., and behind the Central Church the extensive factory of Alexander Morton & Co. Above the point of the same church spire are the curling ponds beside the old road which led on through the moor to Glasgow. Within twenty years of the arrival of the railway in 1896 there was a spate of building of houses and factories in Donington Street and Campbell Street.

THE HAPPIEST DAYS — At the end of last century and the beginning of the 20th, the School Boards of Loudoun and Galston implemented the provisions of the Scottish Education Act of 1872. A national system was established making education compulsory between the ages of 5 and 13. Parochial, private and endowed schools were merged into the state system and to accommodate the geatly increased numbers in Darvel an impressive new school was built in 1904 on Pond Braes (now Jamieson Road) overlooking the town. The photograph was taken at the boys end soon after it was opened. They entered by the west door and the girls at the east. The building still serves as a primary school and as a memorial to the long tradition of education and the excellent town schools of former years.

THE FIRST TRAIN — After strenuous and prolonged representations from the council and the public the Glasgow and South Western Railway extended its branch line from Newmilns to Darvel. It was opened on 1st June 1896. This photograph shows the squad of navvies who worked on the line. The old steam engine, R5, designed by Galston man Patrick Stirling, locomotive superintendent of the company, is being used to carry off soil during excavation of the line. On the right is the foreman of the navvies with two railway employees and on board the driver and fireman. Within a few years as many as twelve trains a day were running to and from Kilmarnock, bringing workers to the quickly expanding lace industry in the Irvine Valley.

A NEW BREED of workmen came with the railway: drivers, firemen, station masters, booking clerks, signalmen and porters, along with the clerks and carters who worked in the goods department. Some arrived by train to take up employment while others were residents of the town like the veteran of the iron road figured here. The photograph was taken in one of the lace firm showrooms, many of which were adjacent to the station. In these the products of the lace and madras companies were draped for display in various seasons for the large numbers of buyers from the wholesale warehouses who invaded the town.

INDUSTRIAL BOOM — As soon as the railway reached Darvel there was an explosion of factory building. The six companies already established quickly expanded and between 1900 and 1914 eleven new firms started up in the town, five of them within a stone's throw of the railway. One of them M.S. Mitchell & Co. was formed in 1905. This photograph is from a later date after the 1st World War when new sheds were being built to accommodate the latest wide machines. Here the first machine has been installed giving a good impression of its width, size and productive capacity. In the centre are the loom builder and tenter with Mr. M.S. Mitchell in the bowler hat, flanked by two weavers.

CARPET WEAVING — The original lace firm of Alexander Morton & Co., had a head start on its competitors. Showing outstanding business enterprise it quickly set the pace not only in lace but in a number of other textiles. These included madras, tapestry and chenille, cretonnes, chintzes, taffetas, dresses, shirtings and waterproofings, either made in the Morton factories or sold in the firm's warehouses. The company had a warehouse or showroom in Darvel, Carlisle, London, Manchester, Birmingham, Glasgow, New York and Melbourne, all by the beginning of the 20th century. By 1887 it also started the manufacture of carpets especially the successful "Caledon" axminster. This photograph shows a carpet loom in the weaving shed. The firm also produced carpets in Carlisle and hand-tufted carpets in Donegal and Galway and remained a commerical success and a leader in the field up until the 1st World War.

CHENILLE — Many of the products of the Irvine Valley factories went out of fashion. The luxuriant and heavily ornamented fabrics of Victorian drapery eventually fell out of favour although of the highest quality and design. The district to its own disadvantage eventually specialised in lace and madras as other lines were dropped such as the excellent chenille curtains and tablecovers which had been produced mainly by Alexander Morton & Co., in Darvel and Hood, Morton & Co., in Newmilns. This is a view early in the century in the chenille department in Alexander Morton's. The machine in the foreground is for stenting whereby the piece of cloth could be drawn out or extended to its proper shape and sometimes a stiffening was applied.

WELL PLAYED SIR — This action photo from the early years of this century catches a player throwing a quoit at the quoiting ground which was laid out on the old clay pit now occupied by Lochore Terrace. The game was played in the town for more than a century before dying out in the 1950s. It was most popular in the 1890s and 1900s when Darvel won the Scottish Cup eight times during that period. It continued for a long time as a game of intense rivalry in the towns and villages of central Scotland, exciting to watch by young and old. The cup games attracted large crowds and the 1st round draw for the Ayrshire Cup in 1913 gives the location of local clubs, although many other grounds existed in the country. Skares v Beith, Springside v Caprington, Maybole v Sorn, Ayr v Galston, Montgreenan v Glenbuck, Byes: Dalry, Troon and Darvel. Challenge matches were also held, singles and doubles, for large sums of money. In the same year R. McBride of Galston played the great Andrew Connell of Darvel for £40. Unfortunately Connell lost on this occasion.

NEW UNIFORMS probably issued at the beginning of the century when the Band began to cause a stir in the musical world and pick up prizes at the contests. In 1904 a new band hall was built in Mairs Road and still has musical connections as the rehearsal room of the Loudoun Musical Society. Mainly composed of local men and boys it attracted during its hey-day between the Wars a number of talented musicians as players and outstanding conductors in Herbert Bennet and Fred Rogan. Like many other brass bands it fell away in the 1950s and has not been resurrected.

"DO YOU CONCEDE?" — At the same venue at the quoiting ground by the railway embankment a match has been closely fought out and a decision is awaited by the spectators. Even the dog in the corner seems to take an interest. The distinctive metal ringing of quoit striking quoit in the clay was long a feature of the town's sporting life. The game of quoits was commonly found in areas where curling clubs existed as a kind of outdoor summer variation, while "simmer ice" was played indoors.

CYCLING CLUB — The great days for the touring cyclist were at the end of last century and the beginning of this, before the motor car claimed the roads for its own. With countless miles of open road and more leisure time available in the long summer evenings and Saturday afternoons, young people clamoured for the latest models of the safety bycycle. Edwardian fashions allowed greater freedom of movement for women to share in sporting activities and Darvel Cycling Club seems to have almost an equal number of men and women members.

HIGH FASHION in the years before the 1st World War. Within thirty years from the mid-1880s until 1914, from the time of the depression in the handloom trade to the opulence of the lace industry at its height the people of Darvel saw great changes. Working people were able to go away on holiday at the Fair, have money to spend and dress in the latest fashion. Here a group of young men from the town in stylish hats and the essential walking cane, have hired a landau and are off on a pleasure trip. The destination has not been identified but could be any one of the seaside resorts or cities reached by train or steamboat from Glasgow to the Isle of Man.

AMBULANCE CORPS – There seemed to be no limit to the number of organisations and activities open to the public when the Valley towns were self-contained units meeting most of the needs of the population, without travelling beyond the burgh boundary. Here in 1912 the local Ambulance Corps puts on a display in the Morton Park. Their smart appearance and efficient care of volunteer casualties have captured the attention of a young audience.

MERCHANTS F.C. prepares to take the field in 1912 not for gold but for glory. At that date there were many minor leagues to catch the aspiring footballers who could not win places in senior or junior teams or the nature of whose work prevented regular training and playing sessions. There was the Churches League which provided some of the toughest football encounters with violently partisan supporters. Others were made up from youths and young men who met at street corners, who joined works' teams or as in this case, the Darvel Merchants, had a common vocation. Slimmer and more athletic than the modern pub team, many of their fixtures were played on half-day holidays on Wednesday afternoons as Saturdays at that time were full working days.

HORSE BREEDER – Alexander Morton of Gowanbank (1844-1923) introduced the machine-lace industry to Scotland in 1875 when he opened his first factory in Darvel. During his life he extended his enterprises in a number of textile and other fields. One of these which had began as a hobby quickly developed in the 1890s and 1900s into a very successful business in the breeding of Hackney horses. His stud at the beginning of the century had over 500 horses. His reputation grew as a breeder and a judge, but he probably foresaw the decline of the breed as a harness horse with the growing popularity of the motor car. He is seen here with one of his many prize thoroughbreds at the Gowanbank drive before the policies around the house became overgrown with trees and shrubs.

THE STREET PARLIAMENT – As their own bosses working in their own homes the handloom weavers could take a breather or a smoke whenever they felt inclined, as respite from their cramped and arduous work. Their badge of office was a white apron, rolled up when away from the loom. They were notorious radicals from the time of the French Revolution until they disappeared as a craft at the end of last century. A very disputatious group of men in political and theological matters, some are seen here in East Main Street in the 1890s engaged in controversy, and holding up the traffic. The gentleman in the top hat was Darvel's "little minister," the Rev. Mr. Speirs. Most of the houses are still thatched. Slated roofs were a recent innovation in the town and as late as 1914 the Council agreed that "all thatched houses should be rhoned and slated for two or three feet."

QUIET TOWN — "The tap o' Loudoun Hill is aye clad wi' weans, Some are pickin' daisies, ithers chippin' stanes, Wi' the cryin' o' the cuckoo and the roarin o' the bull, Ma hert is aye contentit on the tap o' Loudoun Hill." Looking along East Main Street in the 1890's towards Loudoun Hill, celebrated in this Darvel song, the only sign of life is the presence of one man, two children, two horses and three carts. The scene misrepresents the truth as the town by then was a hive of activity. On the right is the new Co-operative building (1890) with its drapery and grocery departments. On the left the two slated buildings are the only two still standing. Next are some of the town's original cottages which were demolished to make way for Jamieson Road.

TOP STORE — This view is East Main Street, looking west. Theekers (thatchers) are at work on the roof of the cottage on the left. Third along on the right is the Townhead branch of the Co-operative Society which was begun as a Chartist Store in 1840 and is reputedly the oldest continuing society in Scotland. Further along is another of the public wells maintained at various points around the town. The Darvel Industrial Co-operative Society moved premises a number of times in its early days. By the 1890s prosperity arrived in the wake of the lace industry and the Society benefited financially. New central and branch premises were built to serve the growing number of members. Darvel eventually merged with Newmilns and Galston in February 1971 to form the Loudoun Co-operative Society.

THE OLD CLIPPING MILL where a new era started for the Irvine Valley. It was here in its premises beyond the Glen Brig that the first Nottingham lace machine was installed by Alexander Morton in 1875, hoping to use the water power of the mill lade. It had been suitable to turn the clipping machinery which replaced the female hand clippers in the middle of last century, but proved useless with the heavier lace machines. A second-hand steam engine from a Galston coal pit was brought into service. This photograph from the 1890s shows it to be an attractive building of fine proportions in an almost rural setting. The immediate success and astonishing profits of early lace production soon led to the construction of a large new mill by A. Morton & Co., at Temple Derval, and a new firm, Stirling Brothers, occupied the vacated building.

THE NEW TOWNHEAD of Darvel was an extension of the town over Glen Brig on the road to the Priestland. In this print of the 1900s the women and children are on the popular walk from the Toll to Darvel Dam. On the right is Darvel Mill, on the left the newly built factory of Morton, Aird & Co., (1900). The lade from the mill ran under the road and on to the Clipping Mill before returning to the river.

DARVEL MILL — A mill existed on this site for over 150 years and was long in the possession of the Mitchell family. David Neil, a descendant, was the last miller. He died in 1928 not long after a fire seriously damaged the mill. The mill wheel was situated in the western part of the building behind the tree and the lade entered a culvert at the wall where the miller is standing in this print from early this century. The remains of this wall are the only stones standing to mark the site of the mill, although the miller's cottage is still nearby. Two small children with their basket are about to "run a message," and in the background is the new manse of Darvel Central Church.

INGLE NEUK — A typical fireside of a but-and-ben cottage last century some of which survived into the 20th century, like this one in the kitchen of Darvel Mill house. The usual features are the swee with its chain and hook for suspending the kail pot over the fire. The ovens are on each side and handy on the mantelpiece are teapots and caddies. The windsor chair on the right is probably the work of local joiner John McMath who specialised in these. Cottage fires were banked up at night and cleaned out every morning. They were only intentionally extinguished when the chimney was swept or on Hogmanay to make a fresh start in the new year.

HAIRST — The district around Darvel in both Loudoun and Galston parishes carried a large rural population. All the farming work was done by hand or horse power from milking to ploughing. The scythe was much in use during the farming year as here in the hands of an old countryman, late last century, cutting a swathe before harvesting. In the 1820s as many as two dozen worked at the harvest in a field, cutting, binding and stooking. A hundred years later half that number might still be required to work alongside the mower. The heavy manual labour bred a hardy race of men and women who might suffer from their exertions in later life, but were magnificient in their prime.

TATTIE HOWKING and turnip thinning were two of the more tedious jobs on the farm. It is only in the last few years that a late autumn school holiday was abolished in counties in the east of Scotland and in Galloway when children were recruited to help at the tattie howking. Last century Irish workers were employed in Ayrshire to harvest the potato crop, especially in the coastal area where potatoes were a main crop. The Irvine Valley being chiefly a dairy and sheep farming district required fewer workers and these were usually found among the women and children in the neighbourhood. In this print from early this century a group at a local farm has just cleared a field in a hard day's darg.

THE PRIESTLAND — "A' ye wha leeve in Irvinedale, And wander to the eastland, To see the far-famed Loudounhill, Ye maun gang thro' the Priestland." The village is now almost a continuation of Darvel, but was once a separate place in a different parish some distance from the town. Darvel folk made the second cottage on the left the goal of their evening and weekend walks. It held the shop known as Gracie's, the friendly purveyor of Priestland wine in the form of Boston Cream. As Richard Tarbet puts it in his poem "The Priestland," — "Her Boston Cream is just A1, And leaves nae bitter traces, It's coolin', nice, an no that dear, ye get the best at Gracie's." The lade from a dam on Tulloch burn ran first to the mill in Bransfield farm and on through the village to Priestland Mill beside the River Irvine. The doors of each of the houses on the left were approached by small footbridges over the lade. The thatched cottage on the right of the road also had a shop. It is the only building showing a significant change in appearance with a second storey added, from the time of this print in the 1900s.

LOUDOUN HILL STATION — The railway line from Darvel to Strathaven did not wait for Dr. Beeching to close it down in the 1960s. It was opened on 1st May 1905 and the line was shared by the Caledonian Railway and the Glasgow & South Western Railway companies with stations at those far from busy places, Ryelands, Drumclog and Loudoun Hill. It served for a while to bring extra workers to the Valley lace mills from Strathaven, but towards the end of its checkered career was used mainly by the farming community. It closed in 1939 and the track was lifted in 1951. Loudoun Hill station shown here was situated at the eastern end of the viaduct, but only the line of the track and the decayed platform can now be seen.

THE GOLF COURSE at Loudoun Hill had only a brief existence early this century. This far from perfect but unique photograph shows a foursome at the 9th Hole. Access to the course was by train to Loudoun Hill Station or by car or buggy. On its high wind-swept slopes it did not survive for long after the formation of the Loudoun Gowf Club in 1909 between Newmilns and Galston. Loudoun Hill golfers could make a rare claim. They played over a site of a Roman fort where eighteen centuries earlier soldiers had amused themselves with a game of dice or kept a look out for hostile natives.

DRUMCLOG MONUMENT — Although over the parish boundary into Avondale the battlefield of Drumclog is significant in the history of the people of the Irvine Valley. The huge conventicle of the Covenanters was held on the side of Hendryton Hill before it dispersed and the armed members of the congregation left to intercept Claverhouse's troops at Drumclog on 1st June 1679. A large proportion of the Covenanters came from the Valley and a number of their descendants live in or around Darvel. The school nearby was built in 1839 in memory of those who died and a tablet on the wall records their names. Up until recent times a service was held at the battlefield every year to commemorate their struggle for civil and religious liberty.

OLD FOLK'S OUTING -- Before the start of the old age pension of five shillings at the age of 70 in 1909 the old folk of the town had to work until they were no longer fit or depend on their small savings, their relatives or charity. The worst fate of all was ending up in the Puirshoose. Luckily this seldom happened in rural areas and country towns where their children, relatives, friends and neighbours cared for the elderly in their own homes. Additional funds were also available from trusts and fund-raising committees to provide an annual outing and gifts of coal in winter. This picture is the Old Folk's Trip to the Bow Butts in June 1909. From this date a Darvel Old Folks Trip has continued without interruption to the present time.

THE BLACK BULL INN was one of the many hotels and inns during last century, reducing to four at the present day. Across the street at the top of Ranoldcoup Road was the Hastings Arms later converted into a dwelling house. On the right is the newly completed premises of the Co-operative Society (1900) with shops, halls and offices. The Black Bull Inn was soon to be replaced by an extension to the corner of Co-operative Shops in East Main Street.

DOWNIE'S SHOP at 16 West Main Street is now part of the premises of the Clydesdale Bank. It was one of the many wee shops in the town which combined the sale of sweets and chocolate over the years with a cafe selling ice cream, fish and chips and peas and beans. Until recent times all of them had sit-in accommodation where a pleasant hour could be spent over the delectable ice cream dishes: macallums, oysters, ladies' delights and ninety nines. The carry-out trade was equally attractive with majestics, nougats, or wibbly-wobblies if you could stretch your resources beyond a simple penny slider or halfpenny cone. Hot meals for three pence or under were plates of chips or peas, a mixture of both in a half-and-half, or a fish supper. Many friendships were struck-up among the youth of Darvel and visitors from neighbouring towns in the little cafes.

ROGERSON'S the old established family grocer's in East Main Street. Although the bulk of the retail trade in the towns of the Irvine Valley was in the hands of the co-operative societies, there was room for a large number of small family businesses, bakers, butchers, outfitters, confectioners and grocers all requiring special skills. Here are four young grocers at Robert Rogerson's shop in the 1920s with white aprons and starched collars. They served their time as assistants. Apart from tea, preserves and biscuits most of the merchandise came unpacked and they had to learn to weigh goods, cut hams and cheeses, package flour and oatmeal, peas, beans, rice and sago and hundreds of other items. Most cunning was the way they cut and slapped a piece of butter on a slab until it was made into a neat little ½lb or 1lb block. Shopping was an interesting experience then with all the town news wrapped up as a bonus. Rogerson's was later to become Johnstone's and then Gemmell's.

FAST DELIVERY of weekly orders and door-to-door sales by pony and cart were features of a successful business in the first half of the 20th century. A well-known figure during that period was Duncan Ross, fish and fruit merchant, who had his shop in East Main Street. Children growing up were familiar with all the horses and ponies which daily toured the streets often feeding, patting and talking to them. There can be few today with the same rapport with modern vans and lorries. Duncan Ross stands at the rear of his cart, loaded with baskets of fruit and assorted children. It is reputed that Duncan's horse could find its own way back from market if the need arose.

THE WAR MEMORIAL – This print shows the outdoor service at the consecration of the war memorial for those who died in the 1914-1918 war. Among the crowd are the Burgh Band on the left and a pipe band on the right. At the rear are members of the Boys' Brigade, while those not sheltering against the houses of Hastings Square brave the elements under their umbrellas. The weather seems in sympathy with the years of grim and sodden battles in France where so many young Darvel men died. To the same memorial were added the names of those who lost their lives in the 1939-45 World War.

TRUSTEES OF THE SAVINGS BANK – The tradition of the thrifty Scot, based on the hard times of earlier centuries, led to the creation of funeral societies in the district in the early 19th century and when times improved to the savings bank movement. Darvel's Savings Bank often known as Gilchrist's wee bank was managed by Andrew Gilchrist who had a jewellers business beside Walker & Connell's The bank, entrusted with the small savings of the townsfolk, was in the capable hands of this group of worthy and dependable local trustees. They were, left to right, back row:– Willie Speirs, William Wilson, Jimmy Browning, Bobby Findlay. Front row:– Tom Boyd, Alex Todd, John Connell, Hugh Barr Boyd and Robert Hopkins.

THE TOWN'S WELLS – Before the installation of a gravitation water supply, wells were sunk wherever a plentiful source could be found. There was a number at the foot of the hill slope in the back gardens of the houses in Main Street, notably the "Minister's Wal" behind the Easton Memorial Church and the "Yairds-heid Spout" on the north side of East Donington Street. The last relic of those early times still in working order is in the grounds of Browns Institute (pictured left). After the gravitation water supply arrived in 1890 street "wells" were erected to provide water until households were connected. These continued in use until the middle of this century. Turned on by the round handle at the side, the water issued from the lion's mouth. The last survivor could be seen for a while east of the town near the Tinks' Road End.

DERVAL DAM

"I daunered on an' daunered on
Till Derval Dam I did pass
And wha dae ye think was staunin' there
But a bonnie wee servant lass."

The dam of the song barred the River Irvine east of the town where the road meets the river. The lade ran along the northern side of the road to Darvel Mill and part of its course can still be seen, but the dam has gone. A series of heavy Lammas floods in the early 1920s carried away most of the dams and a number of bridges in the upper Irvine Valley. Derval Dam was one of the first casualties seen here in ruins with repairs under way to the service pipes and road from the Priestland.

FAMILY GROCER — James Brown was another family grocer and provision merchant in the town trading from numbers 6 and 8 West Main Street. The art of window dressing was still practiced even for the most commonplace goods. Before the days of plastics and laminates the skills of the joiner and signwriter enhanced the shop fronts on otherwise plain buildings, when employers advertised "smart boy wanted" that is what they meant especially in the grocery trade. He had to be smart in mind and appearance and willing to toil six days a week with a half day off on Wednesday.

THE COUNTRY TRADE — As well as serving the towns, butchers, bakers, ironmongers, fish merchants and others also made a country run. In this print from the 1920s the Darvel baker John Taylor is on his round and has two customers at Lanfine Cottages. The baker's van was a favourite with children and here a wee girl stands by, hoping for a snyster. The Cottages were built for the Lanfine estate workers and still stand, but no longer see many passers-by on the once popular walk to Newmilns coming back by Browns Road.

THE STORE VAN — Darvel Industrial Co-operative Society had a fleet of delivery vans and a stableful of horses. Each roundsman had his own horse which he looked after and a van which he loaded each morning to bring his wares to his customers' own doors. The Co-op baker's van was a voluminous four-wheeled carriage which contained every kind of article fresh out of the bakehouse from large loaves to small confections. The van is seen here at the Priestland with salesman Jimmie Valance and a small assistant.

THE LATEST MODEL – It was not until after the 2nd World War that the draught horse disappeared from the streets and fields, but as early as the 1920s and 1930s the motor van threatened its existence. Alex Allan, butcher and ham curer, of West Main Street was a pioneer in this new form of locomotion in the delivery of goods. Unlike the horse the motor van did not remember the customary stopping-places and it sometimes broke down, but it only needed to be fed on petrol. In this photograph, son Alex stands proudly beside the company van, setting a trend for Darvellites to follow.

"RUBY" – Mechanisation did not occur overnight but in the field of public transport the motor omnibus quickly replaced the horse. Many of the early buses were converted 1st World War field ambulances. Small operators were the forerunners and in Darvel, Andrew Smith from his garage in West Donington Street set the pace. Here he is by his bus "Ruby" with his natty cap signifying that he is also the driver/conductor. Inside the passengers look forward to an eventful trip to Kilmarnock.

A BUSINESS OF THE FUTURE – As the world moved into the 1930s the demand for car repairs and fuel increased. Another garage business which opened in the town was in East Main Street run for many years by Alex Lawson and his son Sandy. The garage still occupies the same site, but petrol pumps are no longer acceptable on the pavement and the building on the right has been removed to form a forecourt. Those were the days of carefree motoring with petrol at one shilling and fourpence (7p) a gallon.

THE FARMING YEAR – The farmworker's life was ruled by the seasonal work on the land from ploughing, through sowing and reaping to threshing. The arrival of the big mill was an important event. The steam traction engine and threshing machine were supplied by a contractor in the Irvine Valley mostly by Hamilton's of Holmes. Children looked on in wonder as the great steam engine moved through the town on its way to the farms, pulling the threshing machine and a little cabin on wheels. This was the sleeping quarters for the driver and his assistants. Threshing was a communal affair when neighbours helped each other, which accounts for the eighteen persons in the picture taken at the Lealoan in the 1920s. The women are feeding the sheaves in at the top of the machine and the driving belt from the steam engine can be seen in front of the stack.

A FAMILIAR SIGHT in the streets was the local farmer on his milk run. Women and children went out to the cart to have their cans filled from a churn. Well known in the town for many years was Jimmy Leitch of Gateside Farm with his milk boy Johnny Richmond. He started off on his run at 7 a.m. and is seen here at the railway bridge in Burn Road on a winter morning in 1931. His horse, cart and churns were always in spanking order, with the brasses on each burnished daily at the end of the run. A dairy cow can also be seen painted on the front board of the cart. Others farmers delivering milk to the door were Geordie Smith of Bankhead, Tom Russell of Little Glen and Bobby Clark of Knowe.

ANNUAL VISITORS to the district were the travelling folk in their horse drawn caravans. They followed the same routes year by year often returning to the same sites, finding work wherever they could or selling from door to door. One place occupied yearly was named after them. This was the Tinks Road End on the way to the Priestland. The picture is of an old couple with traditional style tent and cart in the period between the World Wars, before the travelling folk became motorised. They would come and go each year and leave no trace other than the ashes of their fires.

CHAMPION OF CHAMPIONS — Seen in this print from the early 1930s is Sandy Millar of Burnfoot Farm, later in High Bowhill. He was one of the most successful breeders of champion sheep dogs, and around this time had four Scottish Champions. Three of them are pictured here under the cabinet full of trophies. Always a popular sport among farmers it has increased in interest among the general public today with competitors no longer strictly confined to the farming fraternity. Sandy Millar was Scottish National Champion nine times between 1922-34. Supreme International Champion in 1925. Brace Champion (working two dogs) in 1932 and 1946 and Driving Champion in 1949 when he also won the prize as the oldest competitor. He won the Farmers' Competition in 1928-30-34 along with countless other regional and local sheepdog trials.

THE CLYDESDALE HORSE, brown in colour with white on face and legs, was the standard heavy horse in Scotland capable of every kind of farm and transport work. A magnificent animal, strong and active, they were slaughtered by the thousand in the years after the 2nd World War when the all-purpose tractor replaced them. This print from the 1930s was taken at Loudounhill Farm. Harnessed to a box cart it is employed driving out loads of dung to spread in the fields, one of the heavier and dirtier jobs on the farm. The farm worker is wearing leggings for this task, but usually would just have nicky tams — thongs tied round the knees to keep the bottoms of trousers out of the dirt.

TRAVELLING STALLION – A number of breeders of Clydesdale horses had their studs in the district or neighbouring parishes. Despite the name Ayrshire was one of the most important areas for breeding Clydesdales and George Alston of Loudounhill Farm was eminent in this field. He won the premier stallion trophy, the Cawdor Cup, with "Revelanta" in 1904. In this photograph another famous example of the breed "Black Douglas" is in the care of groom Bob Gray in the yard at Loudounhill. Every year the grooms, known as stallion leaders, would be away for weeks travelling round the farms sometimes as far away as Aberdeenshire and the north of England. Another stud in the Valley was run by J & R Smith of Nether Newton.

THE FINAL YEARS of the large studs of the Clydesdale breeders came in the 1950s and 1960s. Over two post-war decades millions of draught horses were slaughtered. This print shows the front page of the cards issued by the Kirriemuir District Agricultural Association for season 1950 giving notification of the visit of George Alston's premium horse "Loudoun Security". Inside the card the pedigree of the horse is listed and the terms. These were £2. 10/- at service and £4. 10/- when the mare proves in foal. The groom's fee was 5/- all giving an idea of the devaluation of the currency in the intervening years. The farm stations the stallion would visit and the times are also given, but not many seasons remained for the Alston stud and even the famous Kilpatrick stock at Craigie Mains was auctioned and dispersed in 1961.

Statement of Cash Payable by the to Constitute a fund as an insurance of their foregoing Rules and Regulations

Names of Farms	Tenants Names
1 Longgreen	Robert Nisbet
2 Wreas	John Whyte now James Whyte
3 Carlingcraig	John Smith
4 East Newtton	Gavan Lindsay
5 Overmoor	John Stewart
6 Crawlaw	James Paton
7 Cronnon	James Paton
8 Neither Newtton	Frances Gebbie
9 East Heads	Robert Mickle
10 Quarter House	Hugh Jamieson
11 Feoch	Robert Aird
12 Glaister	James Mair
13 Alton Muir House	Gavan Lindsay
14 Knewcklaw	Thomas Gilchrist
15 Mossend	James Anderson
16 Broomhill	John Morton
	carry forward

FARMERS' INSURANCE ASSOCIATION — A fire insurance association was established by tenants on the Loudoun estate in January 1828 to cover loss by fire of farm buildings and cattle with the payment of premiums on the value of their property. The society continued successfully until 1841 when by a fatal flaw in the consitution a farmer was able to withdraw his contributions and claimed the interest. It caused two new rules to be added to prevent this in future and to preclude differences of opinion ending in a disturbance of the peace. The association quickly declined after 1841 until by 1850 only two members remained. By then new commercial methods of insurance were becoming available. The books of the association are of continuing interest in containing most, if not all, of the names of Loudoun tenants between 1828 and 1841. The danger of fire in thatched roofs was recognised as office bearers had to inspect all the houses with thatch to see that the chimney heads were "in proper repair and not less than two feet above the turf ridge".

CAMPING at weekends was a favourite pastime for teeanagers and young men when they felt too old for the activities of youth organisations. Groups would hire a tent, fill a hamper and take off for the pleasures of life under canvas. They went to Changue Glen and Pogiven Burn or any other place that would not cause trouble for farmer or landowner. Farmers looked with a kindlier eye then on town boys who might have been their milk boys of helpers at the harvest. Very few discouraged these youthful visitors who required only a temporary camp-site, a burn for drawing water and a little dead wood for their fires. Here six Bachelor Boys are happy preparing spuds for their meal and collecting fuel, while the inevitable football lies handy for an after dinner game.

AT FOULPAPPLE FARM — This print is not about a kirn or other social gathering among farming folk, and the gentleman holding the luggie is not the farmer. The group is the E.U. Congregational Church Choir on an outing. It was taken in 1930 during the depression, when times were hard and trips to more exotic places in abeyance. It also extended for a few more years an older tradition when people would meet at a nearby farm or place in the country to spend a happy summer day in good company.

SUNDAY SCHOOL TRIP — During the three summer months 1930-33 Dr. J.B. Simpson and his assistants held a Sunday School at Loudoun Moor School made famous as the earliest school attended by Sir Alexander Fleming. Some of the local children who attended during those years were John and Morag Loudoun of Low Overmuir; Jane Howie of Longgreen; Willie, Margaret and Ella Ireland of Braidley; Margaret, Jessie and Betty Cameron of the School House; Jim Leitch of High Hapton; Bobby and Dick McFarlane of Laigh Hapton; Bobby, Billy, Duncan and Mary Moir of Dyke; Jean, Agnes and Mary Wallace of Cronan; and Nancy, Jean and Jemima Kenyon of Cronan Hill Cottage. Some can be seen among the children enjoying a day at the seaside.

DARVEL ATHLETIC CLUB — This scene from the early 1920s shows the renowned athletes from the town in the golden age of amateurism. Traditionally professional games were run in towns and villages with money prizes for the first three places until the amateur ideal began to be upheld. With few facilities but much enthusiasm local boys met, trained and competed like those here at Morton Park. On the left is Geordie Nimmo who somehow seemed to be involved as trainer in most clubs in the Valley over a long period of years.

BETWEEN THE WARS the town experienced the extremes of fortune. The lace industry had a boom in trade which lasted into the early 1920s as shops and warehouses restocked and homes were refurnished. From then until the 2nd World War there was a series of improvements followed by slumps, yet it was during this period Darvel acquired a tidy and prosperous appearance. Many advances were made in better housing with the first council houses in 1925 in East Main Street and the replacement and upgrading of old properties. This view of Main Street looking east is typical of the time. At the corner of Temple Street on the right is the Buttercup next to Jack Robertson's shop selling newspapers, sweets and golfing accessories. There is a cart outside Lawson's fish shop and across the street is Tom Paterson's, the fruiterer beside the grand new picture house.

LACE TOWN — The manufacturing base of the town can be seen in this aerial view. The old established company of Alexander Jamieson (1887) dominates the centre. Beside it in the left hand corner is James Cleland & Co., (1907), W.E. & F. Dobson after 1914. Top right are Stevenson, Young & Anderson (1895) and Stirling, Auld (1907). Top left on Campbell Street, left to right, are M.S. Mitchell & Co. (1905), A. Goldie & Son (1912), James McInnes & Co. (1913) and John Aird & Co. (1896). In the centre lies the railway station and goods yard with the turntable clearly seen. Business optimism was still high in the mid 1920s when four new companies were formed, Smith & Archibald (1923), McInnes Textiles (1925), and Smith & Cleland (1926).

ACROBATICS by a group of swimmers at the Dyke Hole on the Glen Water in the 1920s. Youthful exuberance always seemed to be expressed in harmless ways, perhaps because some of the acrobats were happy to have survived the war in France. The town was lucky to have a number of swimming pools in the Glen Water and the river Irvine. A degree of segregation appears to have been practised in the swimming pools as there are the Lassucks (lassies) pool in the Holm and the Rabs (boys) pool in the Morton Park still so called.

A FINE BODY OF MEN — Darvel anglers have fished waters near and far. Based by the River Irvine they still enjoyed their trips and competitions often to the Clyde. Here they are resplendent in fishing gear with rods. Their brake has carried them as far as the Crown Hotel in Strathaven before exposing them to the rigours of the annual competition. Many stories will be told on their return from this lonesome yet most convivial of sports.

THE CHARABANC by the 1920s had acquired an engine and dispensed with horses. With more money and leisure time available it was the perfect vehicle for group outings — an early version of the mini-bus. In summer days it had the added advantage of being able to push back the hood to enjoy the warm wind on your face and fresh air in your lungs. This stylish group could be off to the coast, a wedding, the theatre, a picnic or some other equally pleasant experience in those days of happy motoring.

CURLING — The town has one of the oldest curling clubs still in existence. The game goes back centuries and was always popular among handloom weavers. As soon as there was a severe frost they would detach the large stones which acted as pacers on their looms as they doubled up as curling stones. The outdoor game on ice was probably warmer than their unheated loomshops. The photograph finds curlers playing a couple of rinks on one of the ponds up Pond Brae at the head of Jamieson Raod. Two ponds are clearly laid out in the 1857 Ordnance Survey map. They fell out of use after the 2nd World War when latterly they were used for children skating. Darvel Curling Club is still active on indoor ice and the local players still compete for the Peesweep Medal donated last century by the older Glen Water Club which is no longer in existence. This was one of a number of moorland curling clubs formed by neighbouring farmers.

DARVEL BURGH BAND in 1922 about to start out on a career of astonishing success. Founded in the middle of last century as a loose arrangement of musicians the years up to the 1920s served as a preparation for greater things. Not formally instituted as a brass band until the 1870s, ambition decided, like all premier outfits, to employ a first class professional conductor in the shape of Herbert Bennet. He was followed between 1926 and 1948 by Fred Rogan and they carried the Band to the heights between the World Wars. They were 5th in the British Championships at Crystal Palace in 1922, 3rd in the Empire Exhibition Contest in 1924 and unluckily 2nd five times in the Scottish Championship Section in the years 1919, 1929, 1931, 1932 and 1938. The Band came first in many other contests and during those years was Scotland's finest band, financed solely out of the resources of a small town.

THE NEW BOWLING GREEN was opened on June 11th 1924, marking the growing attraction of the game in the town. By that date there were over 200 members most of whom seem to have turned out with their guests for the ceremony. Still providing facilities for this popular and successful sport, the green is situated between Ranoldcoup Road and Irvinebank Road. In the background are the factory buildings of Morton Brothers, madras and tapestry manufacturers. The Bowling Club was established in 1865 and the earlier green lay north of Donington Street. The modern game is a Scots invention dating from the middle of the 19th century when most of the early clubs were formed. The greens were dependent on the availability of good turf and the invention of the lawn mower in 1830 allowed close cropping of grass.

THE BEST BASS SECTION in the country for a period in the 1920 and 1930s was Darvel Band's which included the brass stalwarts Bob Crawford on the left and Andrew Lawson jnr. second from the right. They were the foundation of the band's success with Andrew Lawson a virtuoso on his Eb Bass. The famous English band Blackdyke Mills were anxious to sign him, but loyalty bound him to his home town. He gave the excuse that Queensbury in the Pennines was "too cauld and windy for his chrysants and dahlies." The other members are A. Lawson snr. second from the left and James Pearson on the right.

GAME IN PROGRESS in 1924 at the curling ponds. Always a good spectator sport if the cold could be borne. Sometimes a brazier would be nearby for a warm and meals were often carried to the scene. The whisky flask if the players were not entirely T.T. was as indispensable as the curling stones and the besoms for sweeping the ice. The number of winters with long freezing conditions seem to be diminishing over the years making the outdoor game a rarity.

WATERING PLACE — As an alternative to a fishing trip to the Clyde the Darvel Club would travel to the River Ayr. This happy group of anglers in the 1930s is standing at the entrance to the Greyhound Inn at Sorn where a meal would be provided by the proprietor, Thomas Brodie, his wife and assistants. This was a favourite hostelry among fishers, cyclists and hikers, with a fire always burning in the kitchen hearth and a friendly welcome for every customer.

THE ROARING TWENTIES — Before leaving the 1920s a new style of transport was introduced to the town. Bill Johnstone, the local dentist, owned the second car in Darvel. He also travelled to Newmilns, Galston, Catrine and Auchinleck on his crusade to relieve the "hell o' a' diseases." Here he stands on the right striking a careless pose with his fur gloves and fur overcoat, compulsory accessories in the days of alfresco motoring. His companions to share in the expedition are, from left to right, Hugh Morton, Tom Murchie, Jimmy Armour on the running-board and Jimmie Ireland inside.

A HAPPY BAND of amateur players made up Darvel Bluebell seen here in 1934 after winning the Scottish Juvenile Consolation Cup. It was a stupendous performance coming top from an original 300 entries. Seen here with the cup at Recreation Park are left to right, back row, W. Wilson - manager, J. Holden - committee member, J. Baird, H. Morton, J. McGillivray, J. Morton, G. Highet, J. Mair, W. Roxburgh, R. Scade - committee member; front row left to right, J. Ross - committee member, J. Cairns, H. Gilchrist, D. Kennedy - captain, A. Morton, J. Thorburn, J. Morton - trainer.

CHESS CLUB – For long a leading club in the Ayrshire League with a number of Ayrshire individual champions in its ranks. Darvel won the Ayrshire Cup in the 1930s, pictured here after their success. The club made use of the facilities at Brown's Institute for practice but, matches were usually played in the Ladies' Cloakroom of the Town Hall. As a side interest many of the club members played draughts. This seemingly simple game was played with such professionalism that a mistake early on could mean an opponent conceding with most of his pieces still on the board. The team consisted of:– Wm. Aird, T. Couper, J. Cleland, Joe Gilliland, Wm. Gebbie, R. Parker, Wm. McBride, Guy Muir, Wm. Gemmell, J. Lister.

FRIENDLY SOCIETY – Members of the Darvel Tent of the Independent Order of Rechabites posing with their chief Ruler, (3rd right, front row) and wearing their colourful emblems of membership. Organised in the 19th century, in times when drunkeness was an additional curse among widespread poverty, like the original Hebrew Rechabites they were total abstainers. They soon had tents in every town and city and ultimately became a benefit society to provide family support in sickness and other troubles. W. Speirs, secretary, is 3rd left and R. Jamieson, treasurer, 2nd right in the front row.

STIRLING, AULD & CO. — The original partners in this firm in Green Street had not been individually involved in the textile trade, unlike the majority of Darvel owners. Both John Stirling and Robert Auld ran dairy businesses in Glasgow. Their lace company dates from 1907. This print is from postcards issued in the 1920s. They were used as their travelling salesmen's calling cards to wholesale warehouses and other commercial outlets. The view is along the lace shed showing the ends of five machines out of the total of fifteen. Lace weavers could stand around practically all day, given good cotton and a well-maintained machine. Without these they were inclined to be thrawn over too many stoppages.

A SHOWROOM was part of every lace and madras firm to display the products to visiting buyers who flocked into the district at prescribed periods in the year. Lace furnishing articles of every discription were available for show as here in a local mill. Very jealous of their product, companies hardly ever exhibited their latest designs at trade shows. Nor were they happy to patronise the local bleachworks, during their short existence, preferring to send their goods out of the district for finishing.

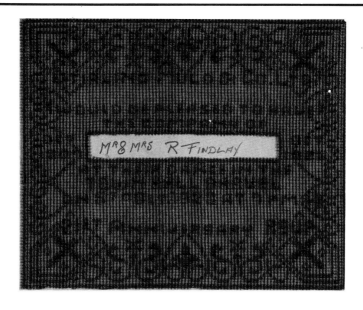

AN INVITATION – What better way to invite guests to an anniversary than a card using the product of your business. This one to the tenter Robert Findlay and his wife has the information picked out within a decorative border in artificial silk. It was worked on one of the very fine lace machines installed by this company which produced quality goods on 16 and 18 point machines. Stirling, Auld & Co., still operate from their Glenbrig factory.

SOCIAL		DANCE	
○		○	
BLESSING, - - - - TEA		1—PROMENADE & CIRCASSIAN	
CHAIRMAN'S REMARKS		2—FOXTROT	
Song—" My Dearest Heart," - - *Sullivan*		3—QUADRILLES	
MISS ELLON DRUMMOND		4—WALTZ	
		5—ONE-STEP	
MR. D. CALDWELL		6—EIGHTSOME REEL ..	
		7—WALTZ	
Song– Selected, - - - - —		8—FLOWERS O' EDINBURGH	
MR. HECTOR COX		9—FOXTROT	
Song—"April Morn," - - - *Batten*		10—WALTZ	
MISS NAN ANDERSON		11—DROPS O' BRANDY ..	
		12—VALSE COTILLON ..	
MR. G. BORLAND			INTERVAL
		13– EIGHTSOME REEL ..	
Song—" The Auld Scotch Sangs," - *Leeson*		14—FOXTROT	
MISS ELLON DRUMMOND		15—WALTZ	
		16–FOXTROT	
REMARKS		17—DUKE OF PERTH ..	
		18—FOXTROT	
Song—"Orpheus with his Lute," - *Sullivan*		19—WALTZ . ..	
MISS NAN ANDERSON		20—ONE-STEP . ..	
		21—FOXTROT	
Song—Selected - - - —		22—WALTZ	
MR. HECTOR COX		23—FOXTROT	
		24—WALTZ	
VOTES OF THANKS			

TWENTY-FIRST BIRTHDAY – Before the severe depression set in after 1929 there was still a degree of buoyancy in the lace industry. In October 1928 Stirling, Auld celebrated its twenty-first anniversary in style with a grand social and dance. The programme gives an impression of the evening when dances were still dances and entertainment was provided by talented local musicians and singers.

THE LACE QUEEN — By the mid-1930s business began to improve again after the long economic depression which had begun in the late 1920s. As a sign of the upturn in the local trade a combined industrial fair and gala day was inaugurated known as "The Lace Queen." Seen here in 1934 with her attendants is the first lady to grace the event, Miss Elizabeth Morton. The procession ended at Recreation Park where the crowning ceremony was held followed by sports and displays.

THE AMATEUR OPERATIC SOCIETY had a long and impressive history of successful annual performances. Formed before the 1st World War it continued through the inter-war years to provide entertainment with its company of talented singers. Concentrating on operettas and musical comedies the Society played to packed houses in the Town Hall. This print is from one of the shows before the 2nd World War with the cast marvellously turned out for a Gilbert and Sullivan revival. The members were part of a long musical tradition in the Irvine Valley which gave scope and early encouragement to an extensive list of excellent soloists who moved on to the professional arena.

LACE OVER ALL — From the first Lace Queen the town entered into the gala spirit making the day memorable for young and old. Practically every house was decorated with lace madras, flags and bunting. A little car which appeared at the early celebrations is seen in Donington Street in 1935 with an elaborate covering of Darvel textiles. Motorised floats were things of the future as all the horses and carts in the district were brought into service. The Lace Queen in that year was Miss Helen Gebbie.

BLEACHFIELD WORKERS — Less well known than Alexander Morton, but a man of many varied enterprises was James Cleland, weaving agent, of The Grange. He was one of the original partners in the lace firm of Hood, Morton & Co., in Newmilns in 1876. Ten years later he started his own company Cleland & Campbell in Darvel. When the U.S.A. placed a crippling tariff of 60 per cent on lace imports in 1890, Cleland started production in Columbia, Pennsylvania, but sold out in 1903. He then built the Bleachworks in 1904 but again sold out a few years later to the powerful Bleachers' Association. His final commercial involvement was the construction of a new factory in Burn Road in 1907. It was eventually acquired by W.E. & F. Dobson in 1914. This photograph of the bleachfield workers dates from 1920.

MILL INTERIOR — The expansion of the lace industry continued from its beginning in 1875 right through to the early 1920s. From then until the 2nd World War it suffered recurring business peaks and troughs. The worst depressions occurred in 1924 and in 1931 when the workers were locked out for twelve weeks for refusing to accept a wage reduction. In comparison with other trades, the Irvine Valley lace industry weathered the Depression and continued to provide a tolerable living to thousands. By the mid-1930s some business optimism had returned. This photograph from the period shows the interior of a lace shed with the front (right) and rear (left) of two lace machines and three workers standing by.

HAPPY AT THEIR WORK are these eight mill lasses of Stirling Brothers. Women were employed in the grey rooms and white rooms and in the offices. They worked as hand and machine darners, drawers and spool winders along with other ancillary jobs to produce the beautiful lace and madras goods of the factories. They were, and still are, the inheritors of a long tradition in textile manufacturing. At the time of this print from the 1930s hours were still long and the work hard, but the comradeship in the various departments sustained everyone through the day, and many friendships were formed during and after it.

THE DESIGNERS — Many types of work went to make up the lace trade. A number of companies had their own designing and cardcutting departments, but there were also separate specialist firms. The interior workroom of one shown here in the 1930s is Smith & Wyllie's in Donington Street. On the left is John Smith and on the right James Wyllie with three of their staff. Women were often employed as designers and copyers and some of their work can be seen in the background. The building now belongs to the Masonic Lodge, but after the 2nd World War the firm continued as Wyllie & Campbell. Other free lance designers were Andrew Parker and A.B. Cleland while two cardcutting firms were A. Frame and Mair & McCartney.

VETERANS of the last war are the members of the Observer Corps seen near their observation post by the cemetery in 1943. When on duty their job was scanning the heavens to identify and report enemy aircraft. By this date the worst of the bombing raids were over, but they could not stand down until the war was over. Other features of wartime Darvel were the tank traps across the road at each end of the town to halt, if necessary, the German Blitzkrieg; the activities of the Air Raid Wardens and the manoevres of the Home Guard. In retrospect they all seem a bit amusing, but were deadly serious at the time. The Irvine Valley was a huge army camp with thousands of soldiers billeted in the district until they left for the invasions of North Africa and Europe.

THE NEW TOWN — Apart from the Main Street, Donington Street and Campbell Street with the short roads running off them very little change occurred in the layout of the town from early in the century. Some rebuilding was done where old cottages were here and there replaced with two-storey buildings. Change eventually arrived with the construction of council housing. A range of old thatched cottages at the corner of East Main Street and Kirkland Road was replaced in 1925 and John Morton Crescent, seen here, was built between 1928 and 1934. Later a large council scheme was started at the head of Kirkland Road, in its pleasant site beside the Glen Water, and extended after the War.

A FINE SHOW — The lorries and carts in the Lace Queen parade were not always festooned with the products of the factories. Sometimes local firms added to the size and interest of the parade with a little opportune advertising. In this case the Co-operative Society has entered its baker's van led by John Lynch as the procession lines up in Campbell Street. The farm and carriage horses had their working lives extended during the War but were soon to disappear from the fields and streets.

PIPES AND DRUMS – The town's musical traditions had many forms. Before the 2nd World War the Rover Scouts had a pipe band and then early in the war the Boys' Brigade. Towards the end of hostilities, at the most difficult time, a band of young men got together in Jimmie Richmond's house in Stirling Castle (Ranoldcoup Road) to form a pipe band. They were given the pipes and drums of the Rover Scouts, most of whom were abroad on active service, the old blouses of the Observer Corps and kilts and sporrans wherever they could find them. Here they are at the school playground: left to right, back row – W. Brown, R. Boyd, W. Connell, R. Coltherd. Middle Row – J. Cleland, S. Lawson, N. Jamieson, D. Ross, T. Richmond, H. Allison, R. Findlay. Front Row – J. Richmond (pipe major) G. Jamieson, J. Mair, W. Baird.

AFTER THE WAR it took a long time for people to re-adjust to the peace. There were shortages of housing, household goods and furnishings and rationing continued for six or seven years. The lace companies returned to private ownership and fierce competition. There seemed an unlimited demand for the product at home and abroad and the town was still proud of its textile trade. The Lace Queen festival was resurrected for a time with all the interest and enthusiasm of pre-war days. The difference lay in the form of transport. Motor vehicles had replaced horses and carts when the parade passed along West Main Street. The familiar view of the Picture House is on the right, but the only pictures seen now on this site are on the television sets in the modern homes which replaced it.

IN PROCESSION — After the first Lace Queen, Betty Morton in 1934, the other pre-war Lace Queens were Helen Gebbie 1935, Mary Hopkins 1936, Margaret Dykes 1937, Mary Thomson 1938, Eva Morton 1939. In this photo the last of the pre-war Queens, Eva Morton is seen in procession escorted by Provost Hutchinson in Recreation Park. In later years the crowning ceremonies and festivities were moved to the Morton Park. The post war Lace Queens were Alice Auld 1950, Mary Wilson 1951, Anna Patrick 1952, Jean Murdoch 1953 and Morag Wyllie in 1954.

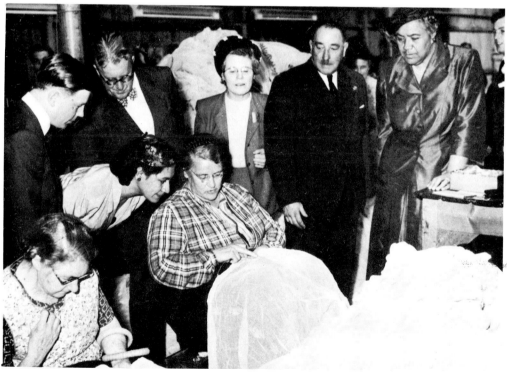

A QUEEN'S VISIT — At the time of the coronation in 1953 a large number of heads of state of countries around the world were here for the events and also toured to many places of interest. Queen Salote of Tonga visited Darvel to see the industry of the town, its product and method of manufacture. This photograph was taken in the factory of Alexander Jamieson & Co., where the Queen on the right watches the work of hand darners, while a lady of her entourage makes a closer inspection. Standing left of the Queen is Mr. Rex Jamieson, managing director of the firm.

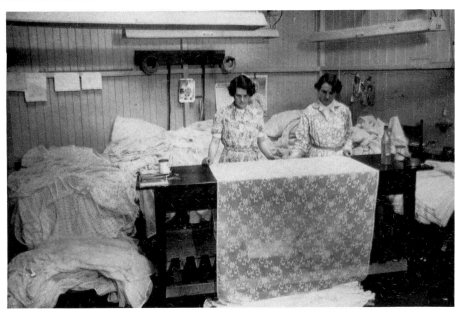

"READIN' THE FLOOER." – In the 1950s the lace industry suffered a set-back from increased tariffs in some overseas countries. Lack of co-operation among the numerous firms, the sale of machines to foreign competitors, low capital investment and changes in fashion led to difficulties for the surviving companies. A few went out of business, but the expertise of the workers acquired over generations remained. Ever since patterned muslin had been introduced to the handloom in the late 18th century local workers had been able to "read the flooer": able quickly to see faults in the cloth in the machine and out of it. In this photograph two drawers inspect cloth over a table in a final check before passing it on to darners for any necessary repairs.

MADRAS WEAVING – The madras loom is the direct descendant of the handloom with steam or electrical energy replacing hand labour. A beautiful, light but more expensive cloth, madras suffered more than lace in post-war years. There was a drastic reduction in the number of firms producing it and tapestry which could also be worked on these looms. Morton Brothers, manufacturers of quality goods including moquette went out of business in 1956. Only one firm produces madras in the district at the present day. While men only were lace weavers, women exclusively operated the madras loom or normally two or more on both sides of a passage as seen here.

SYNTHETICS – In the mid 1950s there were still twenty lace and madras factories in Darvel, but these experienced a decline in demand for the traditional cotton lace. At the same time a new, bright and easily laundered fabric was marketed. This was produced on knitting machines using the artificial fibre terylene developed by I.C.I. The firms quickly installed the new knitting machines, spending over one million pounds within ten years. The earliest nets were plain or of simple design manufactured on F.N.F. machines like these shown here in 1956 in Stiebel & Co's factory. Later refinements on modern machinery can now produce fabrics similar to traditional lace.

NOBEL PRIZEWINNER – Darvel's most famous son was Sir Alexander Fleming. He was born in 1881 at the hill-farm of Lochfield on the edge of the moor, north of Darvel. He received his early education at Loudoun Moor and Darvel schools. He went on to become the Professor of Bacteriology at London University and in 1928 discovered penicillin. Its manufacture and widespread use during the 2nd World War earned him the Nobel Prize in Medicine in 1945. He became the first freeman of the Burgh of Darvel in 1946.

A MEMORIAL GARDEN — Sir Alexander Fleming died in 1955. A granite stone was raised at the farm gate to Lochfield in 1957 and a garden was laid out in his memory in 1960. It was placed at the eastern end of the town by the Glen Water which flows past his birthplace in its upper reaches. The photograph shows the garden in its first location with the sculpted bust of Sir Alexander. Subsidence caused the garden to be resited at Hastings Square, its present position. A fund to provide prizes at Darvel School was also committed to his memory.

THE OLD WATER MILL — As time passes many of the old buildings and other landmarks disappear. There has been a mill on this site since the 18th century, earlier known as the Thwack Mill, producing linen yarn from flax for the handloom weavers. It changed over to saw-milling in the 19th century as the trees in Lanfine woods reached maturity and was operating until after the 2nd World War by the last sawmiller, John Rankin. Seen here in the 1950s the area formed a quiet little enclave by the bridge at the foot of Ranoldcoup Road. The mill was demolished and its yard became the small private housing estate, Bankview Crescent.

SELF-SERVICE — A far cry from the old style grocer's was the self-service shop opened by the Co-operative Society in West Main Street to continue service to the Townfoot and the new housing schemes down Dublin Road. The queue is forming on the opening day in 1957. Around this time the small towns and businesses took up the challenge of easy travel by customers to the supermarkets in big towns and cities.

AN ANCIENT ROAD — Before Darvel's Main Street was straightened in the 18th Century, the old road (see map on page 20) through the town swung south, passing across what are now Ranoldcoup and Irvinebank Roads and into the present Causeway Road. People turning up for the football games seldom realise they are treading on the oldest part of Darvel when they are walking on the unmetalled stretch of road on the north side of Recreation Park. In this recent print the old road is seen rising uphill towards the end of the Cemetery wall, exactly as it was two hundred and fifty years ago.

STRING ORCHESTRA — As the brass musicians of the Burgh Band declined, another musical group sprang up after the War at Darvel J.S. School. Under the tuition and inspiration of the headmaster Mr A.W. Clark and his staff, a school string orchestra was formed. Many of his pupils were introduced to the pleasures of music making, like those seen here in the 1950s at the school entrance. With others under enlightened head-masters some went on to the music summer camps and took part in the regular performances of the Ayrshire Schools Orchestra.

CATCH THEM YOUNG — Mr Adam Girvan takes his class of young musicians over a tricky part of the score in preparation for their participation in the Ayrshire Musical Festival, where the were frequently in the prize list. Left to right are Christine Dunlop, Una Anderson, Bobby Taylor, Bobby Nisbet, Nan Muir, Flora Morton, Norma Goldie, Louise Morton and Gloria Gillies.

THE STATION once was the busiest place in town when the trains brought lace workers in the morning and took them home at night. The mills depended in the early years on the large numbers of men and women workers from down the Valley, and from Hurlford and Kilmarnock. While the Caledonian Railway was open more arrived from Strathaven. This photograph of the up train, looking west, gives a fair impression of the number of travellers in April 1964 a month or so before final closure to passenger traffic. The ticket office, waiting rooms and store rooms are on the left and the roofs of the factories in Campbell Street on the right.

THE END OF THE LINE — The railway closed in 1964 the last train bringing a load of railway enthusiasts after years of indifference by the government the company and the travelling public and a valuable asset was ploughed under. It lasted only sixty-eight years from its tumultious opening in 1896 and had served Darvel and its neighbouring towns well in the movement of goods and passengers. The print is from March 1964, looking east with Loudoun Hill in the distance. A train is standing at the station as the engine reverses. On the right are the goods shed and sidings and on the far right the rear of the old Seceeders Church in West Donington Street.

FOOTBALL STARS — Sammy Cox is one of a long line of star players who shone on the football field at national and international level. He played for Rangers from 1946-1954 and won 24 full international caps, 12 league caps and 3 cup winner's medals. A brilliant player while still at school he turned out for Glenafton at thirteen years of age and signed for Darvel Juniors in 1940. His career followed the earlier examples with Rangers and Scotland of Nicol Smith (12 caps) and Alex Smith (20 caps). The association of Darvel Juniors and Rangers goes back to the time of these two players at the end of last century and was renewed once again when Rangers played Darvel in its centenary year. It is the oldest surviving Junior Football Club in Ayrshire, established in 1889, and over the years has supplied a wealth of talent to the game.

THE WINNING TEAM which lifted the League Championships in season 1966-67 with the officials of the Club. The Juniors went on the following season to take the Western League Cup winning 1-0 over Kilbirnie Ladeside. The team and officials at Recreation Park are:- standing, left to right, G. Young (President), R. Knox (Trainer), J. Currie, H. Mair, R. Carruthers, W. Knox, A. McGregor, J. Gray, J. Frew, M. Gregg (Secretary). Kneeling, left to right, J. Reid, J. Craig, J. Wilson, R. Haining, A. Hastings, M. Thompson. The 1960s and 70s was a period of fluctuating fortune leading up to the dizzy heights of a Scottish Junior Cup Final in 1976. Unfortunately they lost to Bo'ness United.

THE OTHER STATION in the town was the Police Station in East Donington Street seen here before it closed in 1973. Those were the days, it seems so long ago, when policemen were resident in the Valley towns. In the picture is Constable John Milne ably assisted in tidying up by his young daughter. Constable Milne's grandfather who served some time in Darvel in the 1880s is pictured earlier. The station has now been converted into a private residence and a police office opened in West Main Street.

SEEN FROM THE AIR — This aerial view looking north captures the central part of the town. On the right in Ranoldcoup Road can be seen the gasworks and gasometer, Stirling Castle tenement, Irvinebank Church and the Co-operative Hall. Across the road is Mair's School and the large expanse of Alexander Morton & Co.'s factory. Beyond it is Hastings Square with the Central Church and the Town Hall. The other churches a number of lace mills and the station can be picked out in this print from post-war days before many changes among the houses and factory buildings.

BEST WISHES — Drumclog Crescent held a number of the town's prefabs, built immediately after the War to alleviate the housing shortage. They had a limited lifetime and the Council replaced them, sometimes with small buildings on restricted sites suitable for small families and elderly people: In this print from 1968 Provost Frank McLauchlan with some of his councillors congratulate Mr. & Mrs. George Vallance on entry to their new house.

BURGH CENTENARY — The one hundredth anniversary of Darvel as a burgh was celebrated in 1973 with a week of festivities in mid summer. The century as a burgh forms only a small part of Darvels' long history and it still continues as a thriving community after losing its burgh status in 1975. A large number of social organisations exist in the town and the textile industry endures. In this print the Centenary Queen, Miss Jennifer Collins, and her escort lead the parade past large crowds lining Main Street. The Co-operative buildings are on the far-side with Hastings Square on the right.

MILL FIRE on 27th April 1980 at one of Alexander Morton & Co.'s earliest buildings. Last century it housed the carpet-weaving sheds in the widespread factory of the company. The rear windows of the Central Church can be seen on the left and since the fire all the old factory buildings between Temple Street and Ranoldcoup Road have been demolished to be the site of modern housing. Darvel entered the industrial age with the formation of this company and the construction of these factories. It now re-adjusts to face the future.

THE GIRL GUIDES were formed in 1910. They later separated from the Boys Brigade to become a independent organisation. The Darvel Guides are the oldest group in the Ayrshire North Section and commemorated their seventy-fifth anniversary in 1985 with an area parade to the Central Church and a re-dedication service. Led by a colour party and the Brownies they are crossing Hastings Square from the town hall to the church.

IN THE MIND'S EYE – This view over the town will be familiar to the exiles. Looking south there is very little change. The steeples and gables of the various churches, the roofs of the Town Hall and Co-operative Hall, Jamieson's mill and the Bleachfield chimney stand out as clearly as they have for most of this century. The farms, the woods and the fields of the old Lanfine estate look the same as ever. It is only at ground level that many changes are evident in the later history of the town, in the people's occupations, pastimes and style of living.

OLD AND NEW – This weaver's cottage at 106 East Main Street was built in 1797 showing how quickly the new Darvel spread from the original twelve feus issued at the centre of the town in 1752. Behind the near window was the living room, while on the far side of the door the double window denotes a two-loom workshop. On the right is a two-storey house of a century later, when many old cottages had a second storey added. On the left are post-war council houses giving a third style of house building over the past two centuries.

BURN ROAD IN THE 1980s — In contrast to the earlier print showing "The Braes" in splendid isolation, the house is seen among the trees, top centre, but is now surrounded by private housing in Anderson Drive and Braes Court Avenue. On the right are the old stone cottages and on the left houses near the entrance to another private housing development at Woodburn Court and Gilliland Road. Children have disappeared from the streets where they used to play alleavo; jinks; peevers; tig; ba' beds; marbles; kick-the-can; statues; birds, beasts and insects; and the innumerable other ingenious activities of their colourful street culture.

NEW SUBURBS — At the foot of Ranoldcoup Road between the old bridge and the Bleachfield Bridge, Bank View Crescent is on the site of the old saw mill, its yards and drying sheds. It is one of a number of private housing schemes filling up small areas in the town to meet the needs of local people and others who have chosen to live in the town.

The effect the new Darvel relief road will have when it is built is uncertain, but is is hoped it may lead to the attraction of new business and residents when the constant stream of through-traffic by-passes the town.

WEST END —The extension of the town in the last hundred years from a nucleus of one long main street into the large area it covers today can be seen in recent aerial views. New housing schemes, council and private, cover what were once open fields at the foot of the Dublin and the head of Burn Road, but many old landmarks can still be seen. Top right are the lace mills in Donington Street and Campbell Street, and the river Irvine still flows within its line of trees between Waterhaughs and Dalquharn, flanked by the ever pleasant walk on Browns Road.

EAST END – The River Irvine and Glen Water meet top centre in this view. The old Stra'ven railway track is visible in the centre with one of its few remaining bridges spanning Glen Water. Kirkland Park is isolated in its grounds between John Morton and Drumclog Crescents. It was once the home of Hastings San, cousin of Alexander Morton and co-founder of the original lace firm. In the foreground are Paterson Terrace, Glen Crescent and Hutchinson Drive.

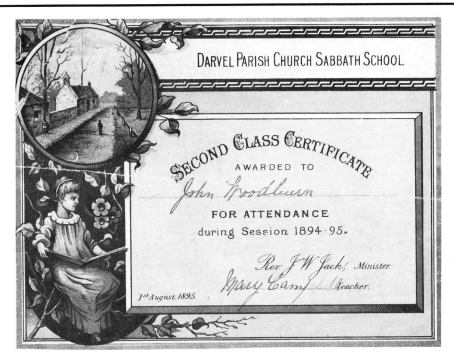

SECOND CLASS CERTIFICATE for a First Class Citizen. This award for good attendance at sabbath school was presented by the first minister of Darvel Parish Church the Rev. J.W. Jack to the late John Woodburn, joiner, 1st World War Veteran, local historian and all round character. Known to successive generations of his fellow townsfolk he represented them in a number of varied roles in each of which he expressed his pride of place.

THE NEXT GENERATION stands at the entrance of the Central Church which held its centenary in 1988. By the door is the Rev. Ian M.W. Collins only the second minister in its one hundred years' existence. The children are Darvel's future and they will see their town far into the 21st century to witness many changes and perhaps pass on some of the old traditions and values.

DARVEL FROM THE AIR
JUNE 1988